TIPS ON TYPE

BILL GRAY

 VAN NOSTRAND REINHOLD COMPANY

NEW YORK   CINCINNATI   TORONTO   LONDON   MELBOURNE

To Sara Ann Teeters, with love.

Copyright © 1983 by Van Nostrand Reinhold Company Inc.

Library of Congress Catalog Card Number 81-22017

ISBN 0-442-22888-0

Printed in the United States of America

Designed by Bill Gray

Published by Van Nostrand Reinhold Company Inc.
135 West 50th Street
New York, NY 10020

Van Nostrand Reinhold Publishers
1410 Birchmount Road
Scarborough, Ontario M1P 2E7, Canada

Van Nostrand Reinhold Australia Pty. Ltd.
480 Latrobe Street
Melbourne, Victoria 3000, Australia

Van Nostrand Reinhold Company Limited
Molly Millars Lane
Wokingham, Berkshire, England

16 15 14 13 12 11 10 9 8 7 6 5 4 3 2 1

Library of Congress Cataloging in Publication Data
Gray, Bill.
    Tips on Type.

    Bibliography: p. 124 and 125
    Includes index.
    1. Type and type-founding. 2. Printing Specimens. I. Title.

Z250.G78   686.2'24   81-22017
ISBN 0-442-22888-0 (pbk) AACR2

Contents

*The medium does not communicate the typographic message —
graphic designers do.*

Foreword

Around 1450 Johann Gutenberg invented movable type, marking the birth of the art of typographic design. Methods of printing and styling of letters have gradually progressed to a point where, today, we have a rich tradition of typographic excellence.

Recently electronic technology has caused explosive growth in certain areas of typography. For example, computer-assisted phototypesetting can set words for printing at fantastic speeds. The basic requirements of visual design still exist, however, and the rules of organizing the elements of type still prevail as they do in all arts. You should learn these fundamentals and use them creatively to help readers understand all the copy that is printed today.

The tradition of type must be considered the most enduring, quiet and effective institution of divine grace, influencing all nations through the centuries, and perhaps in time forging a chain to link all mankind in brotherhood.

Johann Gottfried von Herder

Introduction

The basic fundamentals of organizing type to most effectively communicate ideas will be found in this book. While printing, both editorial (books) and commercial (ads), is the prime end result of this knowledge, other areas, such as television, require the same rules of type organization.

A love of letters is the beginning of typographic know-how. Whereas type may be only a part of the designer's task, it must be handled with the same taste and creativity as other design elements. The contents of this book will help the designer understand the requirements of good typographic design, but space limitations prevent an in-depth examination, and so further study is advised: the excellent bibliography on page 124 suggests additional readings for this purpose.

What Is Type?

The letters of our alphabet are designed to repeat as necessary, to form words and sentences that express ideas.

Type is a letter, number, punctuation mark, or other character used in printing to communicate thoughts and ideas from a writer to a reader. Hand-lettering performs a function similar to type but is custom-designed by a letterer. Calligraphy is beautiful writing of letters formed with a flat-edged pen or other tool. What you are reading is not type, but printing of letter forms that were handwritten — calligraphy.

Until around 1450 all visual communication was usually hand-lettered, written (calligraphy), chiseled in stone, or printed from wood or clay blocks. After type came on the scene, more people learned to read and civilizations using it flourished because of the resulting rapid spread of learning.

Typography is the art of designing with type. Samples of the actual physical form of type throughout its history are shown here.

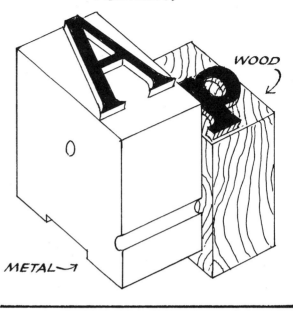

HAND SET
FOUNDRY

WOOD

METAL →

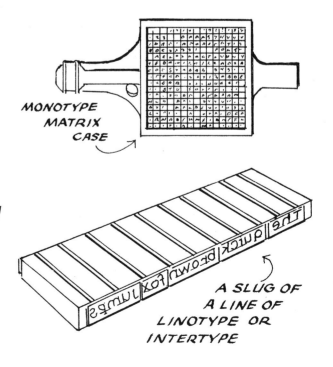

MACHINE SET
LINE CASTING
LINOTYPE, INTERTYPE, MONOTYPE

MONOTYPE
MATRIX
CASE →

A SLUG OF
A LINE OF
LINOTYPE OR
INTERTYPE

TYPEWRITER

SEE PAGE 101

PHOTOGRAPHIC TYPESETTING

DISC
(PHOTON)

DRUM
(V-I-P & DYMO)

FILM STRIP
(TYPOSITOR)

GRID
(LINOFILM)

MOST PHOTO
SYSTEMS ARE
COMPUTER
ASSISTED

CIRCULATING MATRIX
(FOTOSETTER)

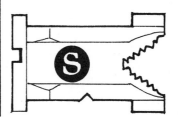

DRY TRANSFER SHEETS

FORMATT No.5370   SPACEAID ALPHABET   TRADEMARK

- AAAAAAAABBBCCCCC
DDDDDEEEEEEEEEEE
FFFFGGGGHHHHHIIIII
IIIIJJJKKKLLLLLMMMM
MNNNNNNNNNOOOOOO
- OOOPPPPPQQRRRRRRR
RRSSSSSSSSSTTTTTT
TTTUUUUUVVVWWWXX
YYYZZ&&aaaaaaaabbbc
ccccddddeeeeeeeeeeeffff
- fggghhhhhiiiiiiiiijjkkklllll
mmmmmnnnnnnnnnooooooo
oooopppqqrrrrrrrrssssssss
sttttttttuuuuuvvvwwwxxy
yyzz$$111223344556677 8
- 899000......,,,--::;;!!??''''""''()

G   Manufactured and printed in U.S.A
GRAPHIC PRODUCTS CORPORATION   FORMATT No.5370

Glossary

Listed below are type terms, which are given at the beginning of this book because they are used throughout. A special list of electronic terminology is provided in the section on computer-assisted phototypesetting.

AA. Author's Alterations; changes in copy by the writer. If made after type is set, they are costly.

Agate. A unit of vertical measurement for newspaper space. 14 agate lines equal one inch.

Alignment. An imaginary line upon which caps and lowercase letters rest; base line. Also a vertical placing of elements with a common lineup.

The color

Ampersand. A character of type (&) that stands for <u>and</u>.

Backslant. Letters that slant to the left, as these do.

Body Copy. The text of an ad or the pages of a book. Type size is from 6 to 14 points.

Cap. Abbreviation for capital, or uppercase letter.

Caption. The heading of a page of type or the large display letters of a title on an ad. Usually 18 points or larger in size.

Case. A drawer, or tray, with divisions for storing hand-set (foundry) type.

Character. One letter, punctuation mark, number, etc., in a font of type.

Character Count. The total number of characters and word spaces in a manuscript to be set in type.

Cold Type. Any type set by means other than casting. Hand-set and phototype.

Comp. Short term for comprehensive layout, showing the exact position of all elements, as opposed to a rough layout.

Compositor. The worker who sets type according to the designer's specifications.

Cursive. Type that resembles handwriting.

Lydian Cursive

Cut. An engraving plate in relief (letterpress) printing.

Display. Type used for headlines; usually 18 points in size or larger.

Dummy. Layout, either rough or comprehensive, showing the arrangement of all design elements.

Ellipses. Three periods (…) that denote text matter is incomplete, to be continued, or omitted.

Em. A nonprinting space unit of type measurement that is a square of the size of the type used. A mutton.

Em-dash. A long dash (—) the width of an em.

En. An en-quad (nut), which is half the width of an em.

En-dash. A dash (–) the width of an en.

Flush left (or right). Lines of type that align vertically on the left border (or the right border). The opposite side of the copy is ragged.

Font. All of the characters of one size of one type style.

A B C D E F G H I J K L M N
O P Q R R S T T U V W X Y Z
Qu & . , - : ; ' ' " " ! ? [ ] ( )

a b c d e f g h i j k l m n o p
q r s t u v w x y z & ff fi fl ffi ffl
( ) [ ] . , - ' ' " " : ; ! ?

A B C D E F G H I J K L M N
O P Q R S T U V W X Y Z &
$ 1 2 3 4 5 6 7 8 9 0 . , -
$ 1 2 3 4 5 6 7 8 9 0 . , -

Grotesque. Another name for sans serif type style.

Anzeigen Grotesk Bold

Hot type. Type composed by melted metal in molds on a line (Linotype, Intertype, and Ludlow).

Incunabula. The first fifty years of printing.

Italic. Type that is slanted to the right.

Justify. Vertical alignment of both sides of text type.

Kerning. Type that sets into the adjacent letterspace to accomplish better spacing, as in **AT**.

Leading (pronounced "ledding"). Space between lines of type.

Letterspace. Additional printing space between letters of a word.

Ligature (Logotype). Two or more letters joined together, as in ff.

Lowercase. Uncapitalized letters.

Mark up. To specify the type to be set — size, spacing, leading, length of measure, etc. Instructions to the compositor.

Measure. The width of a line of type in picas.

You can expand your service.

|← 14½ PICAS →|

Negative. A reverse image of black on white (white on black).

iuſtitiā quā non a moſaica lege(ſep Moyſes naſcitur)ſed naturali·fuit r atteſtatur. Credidit enim Habraam

Oblique. Another name for slanted, or italic, type.

PE. Printer's error.

Pi. Mixed up type, or special characters (sorts).

Pica. A basic unit of measurement for type. 1 pica equals 12 points, or ⅙ of an inch. 6 picas equal 1 inch.

Point. A unit of measurement for type size equal to 1/72 of an inch. 12 points equals 1 pica.

Ragged. Edges of text not justified in a common alignment.

Recto. The right-hand page of a book.

Roman. Type that stands upright, as opposed to slanted italic. Also, a style of type with thick parts, thin parts and with serifs.

Runaround. Type arranged to align with the uneven edges of an illustration or other copy.

Running head. A title repeated at the top of each page of a book.

Sans serif. A major style of type whose forms have no serifs.

Set. The relation of width to height of a single character of type. Also, to compose type.

Small caps. Capital letters whose height is the same as the x-height of lowercase letters of a font of type.

ABC ABCDEFGHIJKLMN abcdefgh

Slug. One piece, or line, of type from a line-casting machine (Linotype, Intertype, etc.).

Solid. Lines of type composed with no leading between the lines.

SS or S/S. Same size.

Spec. A short term for specify or specification.

Swash. A decorative flourish added to some letters.

A B C C D E F F G H

Type casting. Typesetting with molten lead in molds. Machine composition.

Type high. 0.918 inches, the height of all type for printing by letterpress.

Type family. All the variations of one style of type. Bold, light, condensed, bold condensed, etc.

SEE PAGES 104-105

Typo. A typographical error.

Teh INSTEAD OF **The**

U/lc. Abbreviation for uppercase and lowercase type.

Uppercase. Capital letters. Majascules.

Verso. The left-hand page of a book.

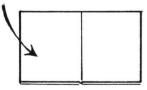

Weight. The boldness of a typeface.

DIFFERENT WEIGHTS OF 48 PT. FUTURA

Widow. One word as the last line of text. Also, a short line at the top of a column or page.

Word space. Space added between words to fill a specified measure of a line of type.

X-height. The height of the body of lowercase letters. It does not include the ascenders or descenders.

A Short History of Type

Johann Gutenberg invented printing from movable type in Mainz, Germany, in about 1450. His remarkable Bible, printed at that time, is a printing classic. The Dutch dispute Gutenberg's primacy, claiming that Laurens Coster, a contemporary of Gutenberg, was actually the first printer, but this disagreement has never been absolutely resolved. Gutenberg used a letter style (Gothic Textura) that was based on handwritten black letter forms popular in northern Europe at the time.

iudeoz ꝫ vniuerſe gentiː et erant conti netures huc modū. Rce antiochus ſi moni ſacerdoti magnoːet genti inde orū ſalutem. Quo mā quide peſtilentes obtinuerūt regnū patrū noſtrozːvolo aūt vindicare regnū ꝫ reſtituere illud ſicut erat antea electūːfeci multitudinē exercitus· et feci naues bellicas. Uolo autē procedere per regionē ut ulciſcar in eos qui corruperūt regionē noſtrāː et qui deſolauerūt ciuitates multas i regno meo. Munc ergo ſtatuo tibi o mnes oblationes quas remiſerunt ti

---

Printing spread rapidly to other countries. In Italy the black letter became more rounded.

tet laude perhenni Lab

In 1470 Nicolas Jenson, a Frenchman who studied under Gutenberg and then migrated to Venice, designed a typeface that he called Eusebius, fashioned after the humanistic written forms of the time. Eusebius was the first roman type style. Today it is identified as Antique Old Style Roman.

oyſes naſcitur)ſed n eſtatur.Credidit eni

Photostatic copy of Jenson's type,

abcdefghijklm nopqrstuvwxyz

Cloister– a 20th century typeface

At the end of the fifteenth century, Aldus Manutius, produced the first italic type in Venice. It was based on local, slanted, calligraphically written forms.

N am ſi pieria quadrans tibi
O ſtendatur, ames nomen, uic
E t uendas potius, commiſſa q

abcdefghijklmnopqrstuvwxyz
ABCDEFGHIJKLMNOPQ
RSTUVWXYZ 1234567890

Claude Garamond, with a
later assist from Jean Jannon,
designed many excellent roman
types in early sixteenth-century
Paris. These beautiful types are
very legible and are classed as
French Old Style.

abcdefghijklmnopqrstuvwxyz
ABCDEFGHIJKLMNOPQR
STUVWXYZ .,:;!? 1234567890

After Garamond's death in 1561
no substantial change in type design
occurred for almost two centuries.
In 1720 Englishman William Caslon
designed the fine Caslon old-style
types, which were inspired by Dutch
types of the time. His types are
considered by many experts to be
the most readable ever designed
and are classified as the outstanding
examples of Dutch-English Oldstyle.

abcdefghijklmnopqrstuvwxyz
ABCDEFGHIJKLMNOPQ
RSTUVWXYZ 1234567890

John Baskerville, an English writing master, designed an outstanding, refined type of exceptional beauty around 1775. It is classed today as Transitional Roman.

.

abcdefghijklmnopqrstuvwxyz
ABCDEFGHIJKLMNOPQRST
UVWXYZ .,:;""-!? &1234567890

In 1788 Giambattista Bodoni, an Italian, designed a mechanical-looking roman type that is very legible. It is classed today as Modern Roman.

.

All of the roman styles shown so far demonstrate a progression of change in the following areas:

1. *A gradually increasing contrast between the thick and thin strokes.*
2. *A refinement of serifs, leading to an elimination of fillets.*
3. *Change from biased stress to vertical stress on curved parts of letters.*

abcdefghijklmnopqrstuvwxyz
ABCDEFGHIJKLMNOPQRS
TUVWXYZ 1234567890

Square Serif types originated in France about 1815 and are broadly referred to as Egyptian.

abcdefghijklmnopqrstuvwxyz
ABCDEFGHIJKLMNOPQRST
UVWXYZ 1234567890

Sans serif letters existed in early Greek and Roman inscription but did not appear in type styles until much later. In the late 1800s European foundries produced the first san serif types (Akzidenz Grotesk, later called Standard). Around 1928 Paul Renner, at the Bauhaus in Germany, designed Futura, a sans serif type based on classic proportions. The letters are mechanical-looking and even-weighted. Helvetica is a more contemporary sans serif style designed in Switzerland; its letter widths appear to be the same.

HELVETICA

abcdefghijklmnopqrstuvwxyz
ABCDEFGHIJKLMNOPQRSTUVWXYZ

QRST anopq
TRYLON

Many other less common type styles have also been developed and are used mostly for display. These include decorative and ornate initials, Victorian, scripts, brush styles, calligraphic, outline, and distorted.

LEXINGTON

ABCDE
OTHELLO

ABCDE
LOG CABIN   RUSTIC

SAPHIR

COMMERCIAL SCRIPT → *ATauv*

TUVatu
NORMANDIA OPEN

IJKLMNOP
COOPER BLACK

AMNOPQRS
BROADWAY

ASTU
PROFIL

FREEHAND

GHJJ aghi
BRODY

LARIAT

WXY
PRISMA

APQ abcd
LEGEND

PRESTIGE PICA

In 1829 William Burt, an American, patented the first typewriter, which was originally designed as a typesetting machine. At first, only capitals were available but later developments included the small letters as the typewriter became a vital part of the business office. A more recent development, the electric typewriter, has resulted in many new typewriter styles.

PRESENTOR

SCRIBE

ADVOCATE

ORATOR

SCRIPT Type

MANIFOLD

LETTER GOTHIC

PRESTIGE ELITE   BOOKFACE ACADEMIC   AUTO ELITE   COURIER 12 ITALIC

SHOWN HERE ARE SOME OF THE STYLES AND SIZES OF TYPE AVAILABLE FOR IBM TYPEWRITERS

In 1886 Ottmar Mergenthaler perfected the first linecasting machine, on which an entire line of type could be cast in hot metal in one piece. Called Linotype, this invention was the most significant change in typesetting technology since Gutenberg.

Around 1946 phototype came on the scene. Phototype uses photographic images to print type. Many distortions of existing styles become possible through photographic manipulation.

Today electronic technology is revolutionizing typesetting techniques again with computer-assisted phototypesetting.

Many thousands of variations of the aforementioned type styles are available today. The serious student of typography should learn of the changes in current styles by constantly investigating new styles.

How Calligraphy Relates to Type

The flat-edged pen was the primary tool used for writing the early manuscripts. The basic styles for roman, italic, and black letter characters were all established by the fifteenth century, before type came on the scene. Every typographic designer should learn flat-edge calligraphy for two reasons. First, most of our first types for lowercase letters have their roots in handwritten forms. A better understanding of these type forms is only possible through investigating and practicing their calligraphic sources. Second, designers must indicate type on layouts, and the method of writing calligraphy is the same as chisel-point indication of type on layouts. Shown below are some of the obvious relationships.

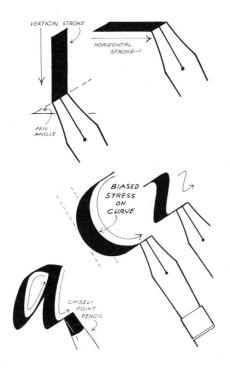

SLANTED PEN

VERTICAL STROKE

HORIZONTAL STROKE

PEN ANGLE

BIASED STRESS ON CURVE

CHISEL-POINT PENCIL

Although the examples shown are for lowercase letters, the capitals can be drawn in the same manner.

gebieten hin ze frankenfurt. die süllen gebieten dem bischof von megentz bi dem panne. vnd sol si

WRITTEN MANUSCRIPT LETTERING AT THE TIME THAT GUTENBERG INVENTED THE PRINTING PRESS.

tis misedia et veritate cu dno meo· indicare michi: sin aute aliud placet· et hec dicite michi: ut vadam ad dexterā siue ad sinistrā. Ruderut laban z ba=

GUTENBERG'S FIRST TYPE (PHOTOSTAT FROM THE 42 LINE BIBLE HE PRINTED (1450).

Today, it survives only as a quaint type which we use discreetly to set a few words for a greeting card or a formal invitation.

20TH CENTURY TYPE DESIGNED BY F. W. GOUDY.

THE PEN ANGLE FOR WRITING THIS BLACK LETTER SHOULD BE ABOUT 40°.

Photostat of Carolingian miniscule written by Alciun for Charlemagne.

One of the results of the emperor Charlemagne's revival of learning in the eighth century was the development of a written alphabet called Carolingian miniscule. From these beautiful written letters (shown above), other major calligraphic forms eventually evolved — the black letter of northern Europe, humanistic small letters, and the slanted chancery cursive.

---

ulta quoque'&bello paſſus laтo: genuſ unde'

Pre-Jenson humanistic writing.

atteſtatur. Credidit enim Habraam deo & leg
quā non a moſaicayſes naſcitur)ſed naturali

Jenson's Eusebius, the first roman typeface.

abcdefghijklmnopqrstuvwxyz

Twentieth century typeface, Cloister, based on Jenson's Eusebius.

Nicholas Jenson's roman type, based on humanistic manuscript hands, appeared in about 1470 and has served as a model for almost all subsequent roman types.

io gli accenda quel tanto dilume col donargli quest
mia operetta, quanto con le mie piccole forze si

Calligraphy by Tagliente, Italy.

Solus enim triſtes hac tempeſtate camœnas
Reſpexit, cum iam celebres, notiq; poetæ

First italic typeface designed by Aldus Manutius.

abcdefghijklmnopqrstuvwxyz

Palatino - contemporary italic type designed by H. Zapf.

In early fifteenth century Florence, Niccolo Niccoli established a writing school emphasizing the chancery cursive, which was adopted by the Catholic church as the official calligraphy for papal briefs. Niccoli had a great influence on the letter stylings of three great writing masters of the Renaissance: Ludovico degli Arrighi, Giovanni Tagliente, and Giovanni Palatino. Aldus Manutius, with help from Francesco Griffi, used the stylings of the times to design the first italic type, based on chancery cursive, around 1500.

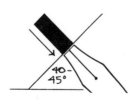

and warmth and happiness

Contemporary italic calligraphy written at a 45° pen angle.

facile a jmiter pour les femmes.

Script written by Lucas Materdot in Avignon, 1608.

Prize exquisite Workmanship, and be carefully diligent.

Formal Script written by Bickham in 1730 with a pointed spring pen.

EXCELSIOR SCRIPT SEMI BOLD

abcdefghijklmnopqrstuvwxyz A B C D E F G H I J K L M N O P Q R S T U V W

Type which evolved from written script forms.

abcdefghij
klmnopqr
stuvwxyz

abcdefghij
klmnopqr
stuvwxyz

Chisel-point indication of type on rough layouts is almost always done in a calligraphic manner. Shown here is the typeface Caslon 540 and how it can be indicated with

chisel-point pencil, single stroked, with flat edge held at a 20° to 30° angle. Almost all typefaces can be indicated in a like manner.

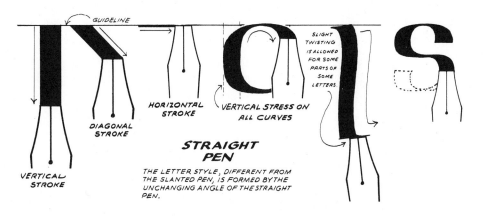

GUIDELINE

VERTICAL
STROKE

DIAGONAL
STROKE

HORIZONTAL
STROKE

VERTICAL STRESS ON
ALL CURVES

SLIGHT
TWISTING
IS ALLOWED
FOR SOME
PARTS OF
SOME
LETTERS

**STRAIGHT
PEN**

THE LETTER STYLE, DIFFERENT FROM
THE SLANTED PEN, IS FORMED BY THE
UNCHANGING ANGLE OF THE STRAIGHT
PEN.

IN REBUS humANISpI REfUSICA ALUCOBISHE

Uncial – a straight pen written style used in early manuscripts.

abcdefghijklmnopqrstuvwxyz

American Uncial – a contemporary type style.

*Shown below and on the next page are typefaces with obvious
written characteristics.*

ABCDEFGHIJKLMNOPQRSTUVWXYZ
abcdefghijklmnopqrstuvwxyz 1234567890

ONDINE

ABCDEFGHIJKLMNOPQRSTU
VWXYZ abcdefghijklmnopqrstuvwxyz 234567890

LADY

ABCDEFGHIJKLMNOPQRSTUVWXYZ
abcdefghijklmnoprstuwy 1234567890

FREEHAND

ABCDEFGHIJKLMNOPQRSTUVWXYZ
abcdefghijklmnopqrstuvwxyz e k m n u thz

EL GRECO

ABCDEFGHIJKLMNOPQRSTUVWXYZ
abcdefghijklmnopqrstuvwxyz 1234567890

COMMERCIAL SCRIPT

ABCDEFGHIJKLMNOPQRSTUVWXYZ
abcdefghijklmnopqrstuvwxyz 1234567890

KAUFMANN SCRIPT

ABCDEFGHIJKLMNOPQRSTUVWXYZ
abcdefghijklmnopqrstuvwxyz 1234567890

TYPOSITOR A-51

ABCDEFGHIJKLMNOPQRSTUVWXYZ
abcdefghijklmnopqrstuvwxyz 1234567890

WEDDING TEXT

ABCDEFGHIJKLMNOPQRSTUVWXYZ
abcdefghijklmnopqrstuvwxyz 123456

MISTRAL

Classification of Type Styles

Type styles may be classified in many ways. Some historians claim that there are really only two styles — the vertical (roman) and the slanted (italic).

Bn *Bn*

Other experts say that there are four styles — the text letter, the roman, the italic, and the script.

Still others say that further classification is necessary and subdivide roman into Antique Old Style (Cloister), Formal Old Style (French-Garamond), Informal Old Style (Dutch-English-Caslon), Transitional Roman (Baskerville), Modern Roman (Bodoni), and San Serif (Futura). All of these were shown in historical sequence on pages previously. Many thousands of variations, called by many different names, have been designed from them since Gutenberg's time. Many more will be developed in the future; and as they appear, you should place them in one of the classifications described above.

ABC abcde
GOUDY TEXT

ABC abcd
GARAMOND

ABC abcd
PALATINO ITALIC

AB abcde
COMMERCIAL SCRIPT

Craw Modern
Century Expanded Italic
Times Roman   **Hobo**
Commercial Script
Helvetica Italic
P.T. Barnum   **Windsor**
Signal Medium
News Gothic Condensed
Derby   Optima
ETC. ETC. ETC.

25

Tools

In addition to those tools normally used by all graphic artists (pens, pencils, T-squares, triangles, etc.), shown here are "tools" especially useful to the typographic designer.

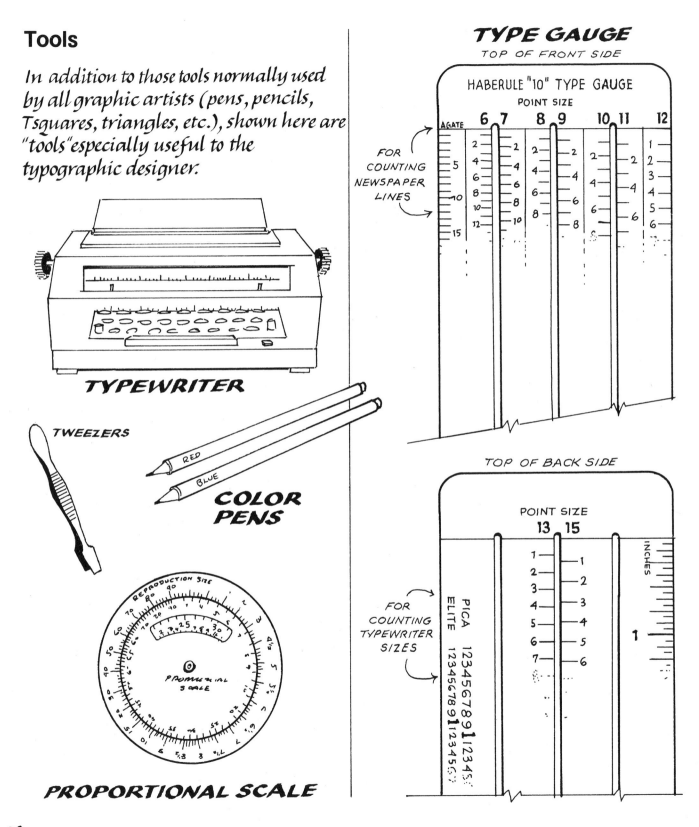

TYPEWRITER

TWEEZERS

COLOR PENS

RED

BLUE

PROPORTIONAL SCALE

REPRODUCTION SIZE

PROPORTIONAL SCALE

TYPE GAUGE
TOP OF FRONT SIDE

HABERULE "10" TYPE GAUGE

POINT SIZE

AGATE 6 7 8 9 10 11 12

FOR COUNTING NEWSPAPER LINES

TOP OF BACK SIDE

POINT SIZE

13 15

FOR COUNTING TYPEWRITER SIZES

PICA 123456789112345
ELITE 1234567891123456

INCHES

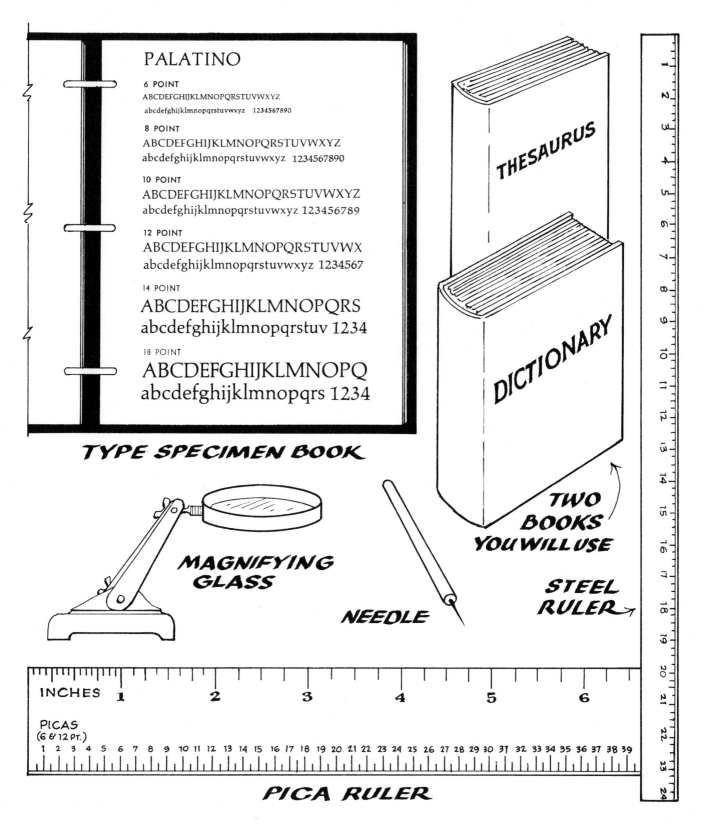

PALATINO

6 POINT
ABCDEFGHIJKLMNOPQRSTUVWXYZ
abcdefghijklmnopqrstuvwxyz   1234567890

8 POINT
ABCDEFGHIJKLMNOPQRSTUVWXYZ
abcdefghijklmnopqrstuvwxyz 1234567890

10 POINT
ABCDEFGHIJKLMNOPQRSTUVWXYZ
abcdefghijklmnopqrstuvwxyz 123456789

12 POINT
ABCDEFGHIJKLMNOPQRSTUVWX
abcdefghijklmnopqrstuvwxyz 1234567

14 POINT
ABCDEFGHIJKLMNOPQRS
abcdefghijklmnopqrstuv 1234

18 POINT
ABCDEFGHIJKLMNOPQ
abcdefghijklmnopqrs 1234

TYPE SPECIMEN BOOK

THESAURUS

DICTIONARY

TWO BOOKS YOU WILL USE

MAGNIFYING GLASS

NEEDLE

STEEL RULER

INCHES 1 2 3 4 5 6

PICAS
(6 & 12 PT.)
1 2 3 4 5 6 7 8 9 10 11 12 13 14 15 16 17 18 19 20 21 22 23 24 25 26 27 28 29 30 31 32 33 34 35 36 37 38 39

PICA RULER

Parts of Typefaces

Shown here are the correct names for the parts of type characters. Always use them whenever referring to the parts.

OPEN TAILS   CLOSED TAIL

TWO STORY a   ONE STORY a

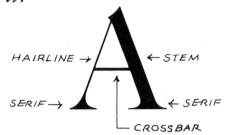
HAIRLINE → ← STEM
SERIF → ← SERIF
CROSSBAR

NICK

UPPER LOOP
LOWER LOOP

BIASED STRESS   VERTICAL STRESS TO CURVES

X-HEIGHT OR BODY OF LOWERCASE LETTERS

WAIST LINE

BASE LINE

← ASCENDER

DROP LINE →
DESCENDER

CONDENSED   REGULAR   EXTENDED OR EXPANDED

SHADED

SHADOW   STENCIL

OUTLINE

SWASH LETTERS

ANTIQUE

SPINE
LINK OR NECK

EARS

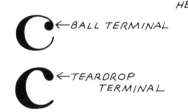
← BALL TERMINAL
← TEARDROP TERMINAL

HEAD →
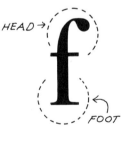
FOOT

FLAT   POINTED   EXTENDED   HALLOW   ROUNDED

APEX OR VERTEX

BEAKS

G — SPUR

ARC OF THE STEM

n

C E — SHEARED TERMINALS

L — HORIZONTAL TERMINAL / VERTICAL TERMINAL

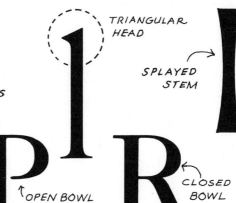

TRIANGULAR HEAD

SPLAYED STEM

1

I

P — OPEN BOWL

R — CLOSED BOWL

A — GRAVE TERMINAL / ACUTE TERMINAL

FLAGS — B

SERIFS

F	**E**	**N**	**F**	**H**	**H**	**H**
SERIFS WITH BRACKETS OR FILLETS	POINTED WITH FILLETS	HAIRLINE SERIFS NO FILLETS	TRIANGULAR	SQUARE OR SLAB WITH FILLETS	SQUARE OR SLAB, NO FILLETS	ROUNDED WITH FILLETS

VOID — O

I D — CUPPED / CALLIGRAPHIC

COUNTER — V

R — TAIL

K

k — LOOP

e

O

W — INLINE

UP STROKE (HAIRLINE) — *ijkl* — DOWN STROKE (ACCENTED)

CAPITALS UPPER CASE — AU ahi — LOWERCASE

→ ft ← CROSS BAR

HEAD FINIAL — m — FOOT FINIAL

FACE THE VISUAL IMAGE — **xpb** — BODY

ARMS

KTY

29

How to Identify Typefaces

Many typefaces are available to the graphic designer. Getting to know them has always been a problem, especially for the beginner. Adding to the problem is the ability of computer-assisted photocomposing and digital systems to distort a basic alphabet into hundreds of variations. Aside from obvious differences of basic styles (roman, italic, sans serif, script, etc.) certain key characters and their parts should be carefully studied. Most differences are in the lowercase letters. All of the parts on pages 28 and 29 should be particularly noted. The one letter that is most often different in different alphabets is the lowercase g. Shown on the opposite page is the variety that exists in twenty-four typefaces. Note the subtle difference in the Garamond, Jenson, and Times Roman on the top line. Also note the Caslon 540 and Caslon Oldface: they are not the same, but the casual observer might think that they are. Characteristics of other letters are also shown to give the reader some clues for further recognition.

Names of typefaces are in small print under the letters

Straight Tail
CASLON   BASKERVILLE
TIMES ROMAN   GARAMOND

Curved Tail
BODONI   CALEDONIA
CENTURY SCHOOLBOOK

With Beard
HELVETICA   NEWS GOTHIC

Without Beard
FUTURA   UNIVERS

Slanted Sides
FUTURA

Vertical Sides
HELVETICA

Middle is Short of Base
BANK GOTHIC

BODONI
BULMER

BASKERVILLE
TIMES ROMAN

GARAMOND
CLOISTER

Cap C at the left has serif endings at both top and bottom. Center C has a serif ending at the top only. C at the right has soft, rounded, classic endings at the top and bottom.

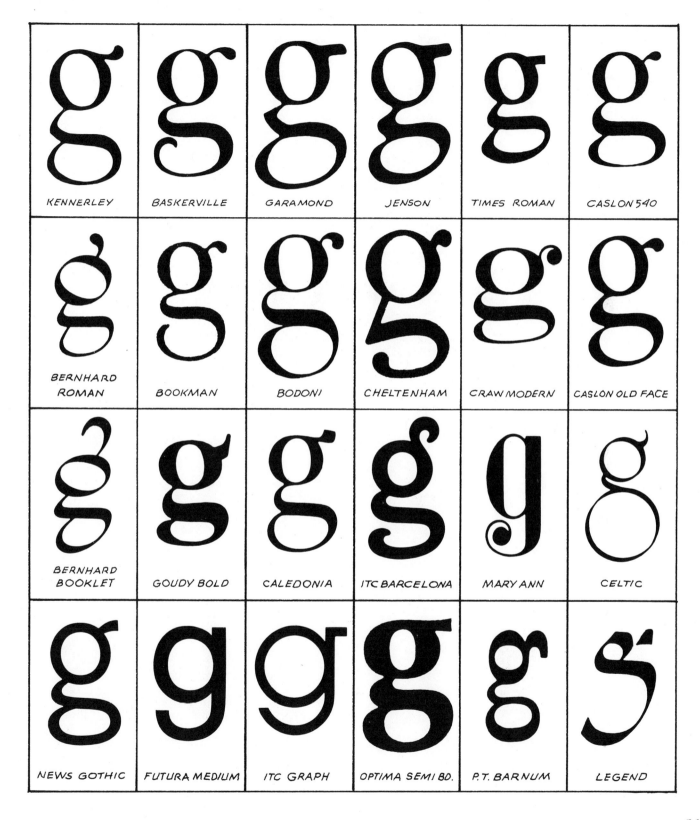

KENNERLEY	BASKERVILLE	GARAMOND	JENSON	TIMES ROMAN	CASLON 540
BERNHARD ROMAN	BOOKMAN	BODONI	CHELTENHAM	CRAW MODERN	CASLON OLD FACE
BERNHARD BOOKLET	GOUDY BOLD	CALEDONIA	ITC BARCELONA	MARY ANN	CELTIC
NEWS GOTHIC	FUTURA MEDIUM	ITC GRAPH	OPTIMA SEMI BD.	P.T. BARNUM	LEGEND

ABCDEFGHIJKLMNOPQRSTUVWXYZ

FUTURA

ABCDEFGHIJKLMNOPQRSTUVWXYZ

OPTIMA

ABCDEFGHIJKLMNOPQRSTUVWXYZ

HELVETICA

ABCDEFGHIJKLMNOPQRSTUVWXYZ

UNIVERS 55

ABCDEFGHIJKLMNOPQRSTUVWXYZ

RAILROAD GOTHIC

ABCDEFGHIJKLMNOPQRSTUVWXYZ

ALTERNATE GOTHIC NO. 2

The top two sans serif types have classic proportions (width to height relationship) based on Greco-Roman and Renaissance cultures. The middle two have uniform proportions and are sometimes classified as Grotesque, a name given to sans serif types by European foundries. Gothic is a term given to heavy, condensed sans serif letters by early American typefounders because these letters resembled those of Gutenberg's first type. All of the above are sans serif.

t t t t t t t t t t

Here are many varieties of lowercase t. The tops are flat or curved or pointed, and the bottoms are either flat or curved, parts to be observed in identifying a typeface style.

e e e e

CLOISTER   BASKERVILLE   GARAMOND   BODONI   CASLON 540

Observe the variations on the letter e set in different typefaces. The Cloister has an angled crossbar. Baskerville blends gracefully from thick to thin. The Garamond has a freehand look, with a high loop and crossbar. The Bodoni changes abruptly from thick to thin and has a straight curve. The curve of Caslon 540 has weight towards the bottom.

u u u u u

CENTURY EXP.   CENTURY SCHOOLBOOK   BODONI   BASKERVILLE   CASLON 540

Here are five varieties of serifs on the letter u. Serifs are not the only way to identify type, but you will become more sensitive to such subtle changes as these when developing a better understanding of letter forms.

T A g e r t a

In any alphabet more differences in form will be found in these letters than in any others.

The Size of Type

All typefaces are measured in points. A point is 1/72 of an inch (actually .0138 inch), so there are 72 points in 1 inch. 12-point type is type that is 12 points from the top to the bottom of the body.

One pica is 12 points, so 6 picas make up 1 inch (72 points). Picas are used for long dimensions such as the horizontal length of a line (measure) and the vertical length of many lines of text.

Sounds expensive!

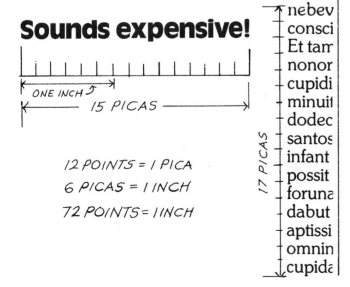

12 POINTS = 1 PICA
6 PICAS = 1 INCH
72 POINTS = 1 INCH

A B C D E F G
H I J K L M N O
P Q R S T U V
W X Y Z & $ 1 2
3 4 5 6 7 8 9 0
a b c d e f g h i j k
l m n o p q r s t u
v w x y z ct st ff fi
fl ffi ffl . , - ' : ; ! ?

A COMPLETE FONT OF CENTURY OLD STYLE ITALIC

Every character in a font of one typeface is on a body of the same point size. A font includes capitals, lowercase, small caps, punctuation marks, etc., as can be seen in the diagram. However, the width of letters varies according to the letter. A lowercase "l" is narrower than a "w". The relation of width to height is called the set of a letter. In photocomposition systems this width is measured in units. A unit's width varies according to the system used.

The x-Height of Type

Different type styles, all having the same point size, may look large or small when compared with each other. This is because the x-heights of the different styles are not the same.

BERNARD ROMAN TIMES ROMAN

72 POINTS BODY (SIZE OF TYPE)

One font of one style includes large and small capitals, lowercase letters, italics, etc. When identifying the size of that style, you measure from top to bottom of the body.

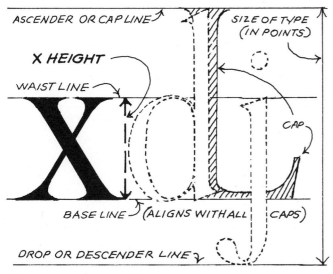

ASCENDER OR CAP LINE

X HEIGHT

WAIST LINE

SIZE OF TYPE (IN POINTS)

CAP

BASE LINE (ALIGNS WITH ALL CAPS)

DROP OR DESCENDER LINE

SKETCH TO SHOW RELATIONSHIP OF LINES IN L/C.

Some of the lowercase letters (b, d, f, h, k, and l) have ascenders, parts

b d f h k

that extend above the main body of the letter. Other letters (g, j, p, q, and y) have descenders, parts that extend

g j p q y

below the main body of the letter. The remaining fifteen letters consist only of the main body of the letter, called the x-height (a lowercase x is one of the fifteen letters). The only exception to these three types is small t which breaks

t

the body line but has no ascender. The x-heights of different type styles make them look larger or smaller, even though characters are all the same size. When evaluating or learning about a new typeface, the x-height of lowercase letters must be noted.

Dimensions of Type

Type has the following dimensions

H M

1. Style.

The historical development of roman type styles was covered on page 13+.

C m *d*

CAPITAL   LOWERCASE   ITALIC

Style can be further broken down to form and structure.

R *r* | S S

CONTRAST OF FORM | CONTRAST OF STRUCTURE

2. Size.

E E

3. Weight.

D D

4. Set — *the width-to-height relationship of each character of type in a font.*

m i

5. Color — *red, blue, etc.*

E E

6. Direction.

R
O
A
ROADS
D
S

7. Texture.

Texture in text type can best be seen in the mass. Observe the variety of textured effects possible in text on the next page.

The design elements of contrast <u>and</u> <u>harmony</u> exploit these dimensions in creating a typographic design. How and to what degree this is done depends on the taste and judgment of the designer in creating his or her arrangements.

Recently electronic technology has cause d explosive growth in certain areas of typ ography— For example, computer-assist ed phototypesetting can set words for pri nting at fantastic speeds. The basic requ irements of visual design still exist, however, a nd the rules of organizing the elements.

Recently electronic techno logy has caused explosive g rowth in certain areas of ty pography — For example, c omputer-assisted phototyp esetting can set words for p rinting at fantastic speeds. The basic requirements of v

Recently electronic technology has c aused explosive growth in certain are as of typography— For example, co mputer-assisted phototypesetting ca n set words for printing at fantastic sp eeds. The basic requirements of visu al design still exist, however, and the rules of organizing the elements.

Recently electronic technology has caused explosive growth in certain areas of typography— For ex ample, computer-assisted phototypesetting can set w ords for printing at fantastic speeds. The basic r equirements of visual design still exist, however, a nd the rules of organizing the elements.

Recently electronic technology has cau sed explosive growth in certain areas of typography— for example, compute r-assisted phototypesetting can set wo rds for printing at fantastic speeds. th e basic requirements of visual design s till exist, however, and the rules of or

Recently electronic technology has ca used explosive growth in certain area s of typography— For example, comp uter-assisted phototypesetting can set words for printing at fantastic speeds. The basic requirements of visual desig n still exist, however, and the rules of organizing the elements.

Recently electronic technology has caused explosive growth in certain areas of typog raphy— For example, computer-assisted p hototypesetting can set words for printing at fantastic speeds. The basic requiremen ts of visual design still exist, however, and the rules of organizing the elements.

Recently electronic technology has caus ed explosive growth in certain areas of typography— For example, computer-a ssisted phototypesetting can set words f or printing at fantastic speed. The basic requirements of visual design still exist, h owever, and the rules of organizing the

Recently electronic technology ha s caused explosive growth in certa in areas of typography— For exam ple, computer-assisted phototypes etting can set words for printing a t fantastic speeds. The basic requi rements of visual design still exist, howerver, and the rules of organiz

Recently electronic technology has caused explosive growth in certain areas of typography— For exa mple, computer-assisted phototypesetting can set wo rds for printing at fantastic speeds. The basic requ irements of visual design still exist, however, and t he rules of organizing the elements.

Spacing

The space between letters of type in a word is called letterspace.

Life on the

Life on the
TIGHT

Life on the
NORMAL

In text type today, letterspacing is tight — the letters almost touch but

should a sample of ty
be evaluated? Any re
sideration must emph
mmediate impact of t
he moment of confron
ween reader and desig
cial. No flaw is permis
he typographer's art do
sist only in the observa
rd and fast rule; it is, o
be, a science of feeling

never actually do. The space between letters of a word should appear to be equal. This is a visual measurement, not mechanical. In photocomposition it is possible to have letters touch, even overlap, but this is never done in text composition, although

touching and overlapping do occur sometimes in headlines. All letterspacing in a body of text should always be the same.

The space between words is called word spacing. Word spacing should not be too tight, or the words will run together and become hard to read. Correct word spacing is shown here.

tap to land. The sun dipped behind the horizon,
quiring looks passed from one guest to another;
hand on the door-knob and had turned it; waite
away his hand and let the knob turn back again

TOO LITTLE

Bixby pulled the cord, and two deep, mel
big bell floated off on the night. Then a
note was struck. The watchman's voice f
hurricane deck: —

TOO MUCH

the bend. More looks were exchanged, and n
miration — but no words. Insensibly the men
Mr. Bixby, as the sky darkened and one or t
The dead silence and sense of waiting becam

JUST RIGHT

The space between lines of type is called leading (ledding). This is also a visual measurement. Leading tables for various lengths of lines are *shown here for guidance.*

LEADING TABLE FOR TEXT		
TYPE SIZE	MINIMUM LEADING	MAXIMUM LEADING
6 PT.	SOLID	1 POINT
8 PT.	SOLID	2 POINT
10 PT.	SOLID to 2 POINT	4 POINT
11 PT.	1 POINT	4 POINT
12 PT.	2 POINT	6 POINT
14 PT.	3 POINT	8 POINT

Word spacing should never be greater than leading.

An em is another unit of space. It is a nonprinting square that is the size of the type. An en is half of an em measured horizontally; vertically, it is the same size as an em. Parts of ems (4 to an em, 3 to an em, etc.) were used in spacing metal type.

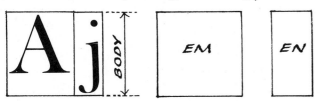

In photocomposition, units are used for letterspacing, word spacing, and leading.

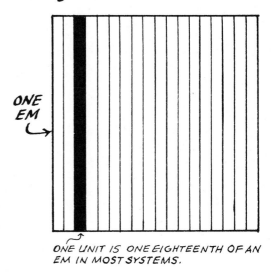

ONE EM

ONE UNIT IS ONE EIGHTEENTH OF AN EM IN MOST SYSTEMS.

There are 14 agate lines to 1 inch. Agate lines are used to give column depths (for example, 1 col x 28 agate lines = column width by 2 inches deep).

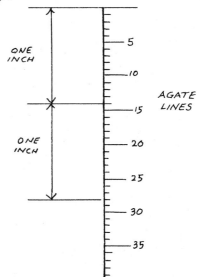

ONE INCH

ONE INCH

AGATE LINES

Text and Display

The pages of a book (editorial) and the descriptive lines of type under a headline in an ad (commercial) are usually composed of type designed for easy reading called text type or body copy. When designing lines of text, the style and size of the type, the length of the lines, and the spacing of letters and words and between lines must be determined. Text type is usually 14 points or smaller.

HEADLINE ⟶

Time to RE-TIRE?

Lorem ipsum dolor sit amet elit, sed diam nonnumy eiu labore et dolore magna alic enim ad minimim veniami ullamcorpor suscipit laboris commodo consequat. Duis in reprehenderit in voluptate consequat, vel illum dolore vero eos et accusam et justo blandit praesent lupatum molestais exceptur

⟵ TEXT

The type used for headlines in ads and headings on pages of a book is called display. These types are larger and can be bolder and more decorative than text type. A much greater number of typefaces have been designed for display than for text. Display types are usually 14 points or larger, sometimes much larger, as in a poster.

Design of Text

When designing text, the following guidelines will help make your text most readable

Large areas of text set in all capitals take more time to read than text set in lowercase.

WOULD THAT WE COULD AT ONCE PAINT WITH THE EYES! IN THE LONG WAY FROM THE EYE THROUGH THE ARM TO THE PENCIL, HOW MUCH IS LOST!

Would that we could at once paint with the eyes! In the long way from the eye through the arm to the pencil, how much is lost!

Readers prefer roman to italic type in large areas.

Recently electronic technology has caused explosive growth in certain areas of typog raphy— For example, computer-assisted p hototypesetting can set words for printing at fantastic speeds. The basic requiremen ts of visual design still exist, however, and

Recently electronic technology has caused explosive growth in certain areas of typography— For exa mple, computer-assisted phototypesetting can set wo rds for printing at fantastic speeds. The basic requ irements of visual design still exist, however, and t he rules of organizing the elements.

Save italics for emphasis or lead-ins to paragraphs.

Because of new technologies of typesetting, the job of choos- ing type and deciding on *the methods by which it is set* is more complicated today than it used to be. There was a time not

How should a sample of typography be evaluated? Any realistic considera tion must emphasize the immediate

Use but a few faces for your text. Some of the best designers use just one or two. Roman styles are less tiring to the eye, but sans serifs and square serifs are acceptable if copy is not too long.

Type printed in reverse slows reading considerably.

Recently electronic technology ha s caused explosive growth in certa in areas of typography— For exam ple, computer-assisted phototypes etting can set words for printing a t fantastic speeds. The basic requi rements of visual design still exis t, however, and the rules of organ

Recently electronic technology ha s caused explosive growth in certa in areas of typography— For exam ple, computer-assisted phototypes etting can set words for printing a t fantastic speeds. The basic requi rements of visual design still exis t, however, and the rules of organ

How should a sample of ize the immediate impa signer is crucial. No fla he observation of hard a w, a ministry to the eye ertain train of meditati er who is not gifted wit m precisely to the same he act

Margins of white space around your copy do not affect speed of reading text, but surrounding text with space is a good practice because it invites reading and gives some flexibility in copy-fitting to your layout.

typography be evaluated? ct of the type. The momen w is permissible, for the ty ind fast rule; it is, or ought more than to the mind. An n, and convinces one of t h the fine sympathies of t general doctrines that ap

Dull-coated or antique finish on paper is better than high-gloss-coated paper, which may interfere with readability.

ensively in fine bookwork because of their readability and because they print well on book paper. Advertising designers who wish to give their copy a feeling of age and tradition often use these faces. Since certain old style faces have an app

is one of more than two hundred similar organizations throughout the

Very short and very long text lines are hard to read. The table shown here will help you determine length of line of text.

LENGTH OF LINE TABLE

TYPE SIZE	MAXIMUM (PICAS)	MINIMUM (PICAS)
6 pt.	10	8
8 pt.	13	9
10 pt.	16	13
11 pt.	18	13
12 pt.	21	14
14 pt.	24	18
18 pt.	30	24

Sixty to seventy characters, or seven to ten words, per line are ideal for books.

The entire body of text should have an overall even tone of gray. To test this, hold a proof of it at arm's length and squint slightly while observing it. Does it have dark and light areas? It shouldn't have. Observe it upside down.

knowledge, and marvel-
lous facility, compared
a pilot's massed knowl-
edge of the Mississippi
and his marvellous facility
in the handling of it. I
make this comparison
deliberately, and believe
I am not expanding the
truth when I do it. Many
will think my figure too

When a very small type size is required, choose one with a large x-height.

dent, simil tempor sunt in
mollit anim id est laborum et
dereud facilis est er expedit
tempor cum soluta nobis el.

elit, sed diam nonnumy eiu
labore et dolore magna
enim ad minimim veniami
ullamcorpor suscipit laboris

BOTH STYLES ABOVE ARE 14 Pt. THE LOWER LOOKS LARGER.

Do not indent the first line of the first paragraph following a headline. Do indent all other first lines of paragraphs.

Keep word spacing and letterspace tight. Specify "tight" when ordering photocomposed text.

Keeping paragraphs short, especially the first one, improves legibility.

Paragraphs of varied lengths sustain a reader's interest.

Uniform word spacing improves legibility.

Do not print paragraphs over tint blocks or illustrations, as this reduces legibility.

quod a impedit anim id quo
possim omnis es voluptas ass
dolor repellend. Temporem
office debit aut tum rerum
ut er repudiand sint et molestia
itaque earud rerum hic tene

Most printed communications have a typeface that is most appropriate to its message. If none exists, simply choose a very legible face.

AQRSTU apqrstu

24 PT. CASLON 540. "WHEN IN DOUBT USE CASLON." ANON

Old style text styles look better on antique-finish paper, whereas modern styles are better on glossy-coated paper.

ADE ahijk

36 PT. GOUDY OLD STYLE

AW avwxyz

36 PT. BODONI BOOK

Bodoni said, "Use one-third of the text type size as the leading in text type."

If text for an ad is adjacent to editorial matter in a book or magazine, make the text size larger than the editorial type.

When children and older folks are to read your copy, keep the size of type relatively large.

Lines of sans serif text should always be leaded.

sively in fine bookwork because of their reada
bility and because they print well on book pap
er. Advertising designers who wish to give thei
r copy a feeling of age and tradition often use
these faces. Since certain old-style faces have

10 PT. HELVETICA   SET SOLID

sively in fine bookwork because of their reada
bility and because they print well on book pap
er. Advertising designers who wish to give thei
r copy a feeling of age and tradition often use
these faces. Since certain old-style faces have

10 PT. HELVETICA   LEADED 1 P.T.

Word space should never be more than leading.

Text set in blackletter types should always be packed, with little or no letterspacing.

aber steht über
der Kunst und dem Gegen-
stande: über jener, da er sie zu
seinen Zwecken braucht, über
diesem, weil er ihn nach eigner
Weise behandelt.

ABOVE TYPE IS KLINGSPORSCHRIFT
DESIGNED BY RUDOLF KOCH.

5000-28	5100-34	5200-27	5300-42	5400-31
5001-28	5101-34	5201-27	5301-42	5401-31
5002-28	5102-34	5202-27	5302-42	5402-31
5003-28	5103-34	5203-19	5303-41	5403-31
5004-28	5104-34	5204-53	5304-41	5404-31
5005-28	5105-34	5205	5305-41	5405-31
5006-28	5106-42	5206-44	5306-41	5406-47
5007-28	5107-46	5207-24	5307-41	5407-47
5008-28	5108	5208-20	5308-41	5408-38
5009-28	5109	5209-20	5309	5409-38
5010	5110	5210-27	5310	5410-38
5011	5111-33	5211-27	5311-42	5411-38
5012	5112-33	5212-27	5312	5412-51
5013	5113-33	5213-27	5313-42	5413-51
5014-28	5114-33	5214-27	5314-42	5414-51
5015-29	5115-33	5215-26	5315-40	5415-51
5016	5116-33	5216-26	5316-40	5416-39
5017	5117-33	5217-26	5317-40	5417-39
5018-29	5118	5218-26	5318-40	5418-39
5019-29	5119	5219-26	5319	5419-39
5020-53	5120	5220-26	5320-40	5420-39
5021-53	5121-33	5221-26	5321	5421
5022-53	5122-33	5222-26	5322-43	5422-40
5023-49	5123-33	5223-26	5323-25	5423-40
5024-49	5124-33	5224-26	5324-12	5424-40

If you must have a word positioned vertically, center the letters on a common center line

When specifying the text type on your manuscript, give the complete name of the type. For example, write Futura Demibold Condensed if that is what you want — not just Futura.

Never use type styles that are the same as a competitor's. If you know what he uses, try some other style.

The larger the text type, the lighter its weight can be.

For copy with many figures, such as a company financial report, use lining numerals that are all the same height. Never use old-style nonaligning numerals for such items.

If clippings to be set accompany your manuscript, paste them onto standard 8½ by 11 sheets, the same size as the rest of the manuscript.

When you count characters to estimate fitting of text type on any electronic system, be sure that your characters-per-pica count is <u>exactly</u> the same as the system that will set it.

When counting characters of text type, do not forget to count one count for spaces between words and two counts for capitals.

Avoid thin-line styles for reverse printings.

Avoid thin-line type when the type is to be printed in a color that requires two impressions.

If hand-lettering is used, it should complement the text style or be in contrast to it.

Always send a copy of the layout along with your manuscript specifications.

ntiam, quid est cur verear possing accommodare no-ante cum memorite it tum-amice et nebevol, olestias-ad augendas cum conscien

Do not have more than two end-of-line hyphens in a row. Avoid hyphenating any word.

If you have an unusually large amount of copy for text and want to save space, use paragraph marks to indicate new paragraphs.

For text types that have small bodies but long ascenders and descenders, you may want minus leading, which is possible with phototype-setting.

When paragraphs of text type do not quite fit because of some unforseen reason, the type can be repositioned as shown below. Cut the paragraphs apart, leave extra space between — them, and reposition them to fit the original space. If there is space around the text in the layout, you might simply photostat the text to fit, as shown below.

The designer was able to bring a whole new background and a new set of influences to the printed page. "He could "draw" a page. There was more flexibility in the use of a pencil than in the manipulation of a metal form. It became a new medium for the designer.

Under the twin impact of the functionalism of the Bauhaus and the practical demands of American business, the designer was beginning to learn to use the combination of word and image to communicate more effectively.

Under the influence of the modern painters, he became aware (perhaps too aware) of the textural qualities and color values of type as an element of design.

And surely a dominating influence on American typography in the pre-war years was exerted by the journalists.

Newspapers and magazines were the primary media of mass communication.

The skillful development of the use of headline and picture was a far more prevalent influence than the European poster. The newspaper taught us speed in communication. Everyone knew instinctively what the journalists had reduced to a formula: that if you read a headline, a picture, and the first three paragraphs of any story you would know all the essential facts.

The magazine communicated at a more leisurely pace and could be more provocative since it addressed a more selective audience. Because the magazine dealt more in concepts than in news it was far more imaginative. There was more opportunity here to design within the framework of the two-page spread. But still, the devices that bore the main burden of interesting the reader were the "terrific headline" and the "wonderful picture."

The designer was able to bring a whole new background and a new set of influences to the printed page. "He could "draw" a page. There was more flexibility in the use of a pencil than in the manipulation of a metal form. It became a new medium for the designer.

Under the twin impact of the functionalism of the Bauhaus and the practical demands of American business, the designer was beginning to learn to use the combination of word and image to communicate more effectively.

Under the influence of the modern painters, he became aware (perhaps too aware) of the textural qualities and color values of type as an element of design.

And surely a dominating influence on American typography in the pre-war years was exerted by the journalists.

Newspapers and magazines were the primary media of mass communication.

The skillful development of the use of headline and picture was a far more prevalent influence than the European poster. The newspaper taught us speed in communication. Everyone knew instinctively what the journalists had reduced to a formula: that if you read a headline, a picture, and the first three paragraphs of any story you would know all the essential facts.

The magazine communicated at a more leisurely pace and could be more provocative since it addressed a more selective audience. Because the magazine dealt more in concepts than in news it was far more imaginative. There was more opportunity here to design within the framework of the two-page spread. But still, the devices that bore the main burden of interesting the reader were the "terrific headline" and the "wonderful picture."

The designer was able to bring a whole new background and a new set of influences to the printed page. "He could "draw" a page. There was more flexibility in the use of a pencil than in the manipulation of a metal form. It became a new medium for the designer.

Under the twin impact of the functionalism of the Bauhaus and the practical demands of American business, the designer was beginning to learn to use the combination of word and image to communicate more effectively.

Under the influence of the modern painters, he became aware (perhaps too aware) of the textural qualities and color values of type as an element of design.

And surely a dominating influence on American typography in the pre-war years was exerted by the journalists.

Newspapers and magazines were the primary media of mass communication.

The skillful development of the use of headline and picture was a far more prevalent influence than the European poster. The newspaper taught us speed in communication. Everyone knew instinctively what the journalists had reduced to a formula: that if you read a headline, a picture, and the first three paragraphs of any story you would know all the essential facts.

The magazine communicated at a more leisurely pace and could be more provocative since it addressed a more selective audience. Because the magazine dealt more in concepts than in news it was far more imaginative. There was more opportunity here to design within the framework of the two-page spread. But still, the devices that bore the main burden of interesting the reader were the "terrific headline" and the "wonderful picture."

TYPE INDICATION OF TEXT ON ORIGINAL LAYOUT

TYPE PROOF WHICH IS NOT THE SAME DEPTH AS LAYOUT

SPACE ADDED BETWEEN PARAGRAPHS TO FIT

PHOTOSTAT ENLARGED FROM PROOF TO FIT

If you know how many characters per line your copy will take, have the typist try to hold to that number in typing the final manuscript.

The character count method is the surest and most accurate system of copy-fitting.

When marking up your copy on the manuscript, write very legibly.

Avoid hyphenating words in text.

When in doubt about what size to set text type, first cast it in a size smaller than you might have originally visualized it.

Remember — the best time to edit copy is before it goes to the compositor.

Keep all liquids away from the manuscript (coffee, rubber cement, etc.).

Brackets and parentheses were designed to center on lowercase letters. They will have to be repositioned if used with caps.

(TYPE) (type)

An ideal length of line is about forty characters. Less than thirty or more than fifty characters is to be avoided.

None of the above guidelines are absolute — part of the fun in designing with type is to try something new. But when you do try something innovative, be sure that readers will comprehend your text and not simply get ecstatic about a new artistic effort that may not be readable.

Choose lighter faced type for gravure printing; it will heavy-up when printed.

Brooklyn Dodgers

ENLARGED PHOTOSTAT OF TYPE PRINTED BY GRAVURE

Allow extra leading between paragraphs of continuous copy.

The history of writing on paper began in China about the year 105 A.D. Before that, various peoples of the world had employed papyrus, parchment, cloth, bark, and stone on which to communicate their written messages. By the first century A.D., calligraphy, or writing, had gained such importance in China that a practical writing surface had become a necessity.

Over six centuries elapsed before paper making found its way westward, following the caravan routes from the Pacific Ocean to the Southern Mediterranean. From Egypt and Morocco it reached the European continent by the middle of the 12th century. Actual paper mills appeared in Italy by 1276 and in France by 1348. By 1350, the use of paper for literary purposes was firmly established.

America, in her early days, imported paper from England where it had been made since the 15th century. By 1690, the first American paper producer made an appearance. With the beginning of the American Revolution, and the impossibility of receiving imports from England, a great paper shortage arose in America.

Surprising as it may seem, despite paper's long history, it was not until the mid-nineteenth century with (1) the first papermaking machines and (2) the use of wood pulp in addition to cotton fiber pulp, that the age of economical mass-produced paper became a

es are used
book paper.
ey print well
nd decorum,
nd dignified

RIGHT MARGIN OF JUSTFIED TYPE ——→

Many designers hang punctuation marks in justified blocks of text.

vely in fine bookwork because of their readability and be cause they print well on book paper. Advertising designe rs who wish to give their copy a feeling of age and traditi on often use these faces. Since certain old style faces have an appearance of antiquity and decorum, they are particu

ONE POINT LEADED

ly in fine bookwork because of their readability and because they print well on book paper. Advertising designers who wish to give their copy a feeling of a ge and tradition often use these faces. Since certain old-style faces have an appearance of antiquity and

TWO POINT LEADED

Typefaces with short ascenders and descenders need more leading than type of the same size with long ascenders and descenders.

The quick brown fox jumps over the lazy dog

The quick brown fox jumps over the lazy

A narrow text type needs less word space, whereas a wide type needs more word space.

Some designers use the following
rules of thumb when designing
text type line widths:

1. Point size of the type times 2
equals the length of line in picas.

Most old-style types are used extensively in fine bookw
ity and because they print well on book paper. Advertisi
e their copy a feeling of age and tradition often use thes

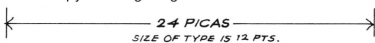

←————————— 24 *PICAS* ————————→
SIZE OF TYPE IS 12 PTS.

2. The length of line, in picas, is
the width of the alphabet from a to z
times 1½.

Most old-style types are used extensively i
heir readability and because they print wel
designers who wish to give their copy a feel

←————————— 21¾, OR 22, *PICAS* ————————→
abcdefghijklmnopqrstuvwxyz
ALPHABET LENGTH OF 14 PT. TYPE IS 14½ PICAS

Heavy (bold) type needs more leading
than light types.

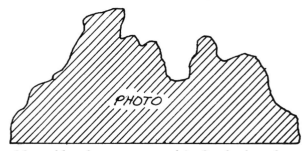

Most old style types are used in fine bookwork

Do not break words at the end of text
lines. Entire books have been printed
without a single broken word.

Always include a caption with a
photo. Captions are read more often
than body copy is.

The following styles are most often used for text by graphic designers today. These are text typefaces you should know. They are in addition to others already shown (Garamond, Baskerville, Caslon, etc.).

ABCDEFGHIJKLMNOPQRSTUVWXYZ

abcdefghijklmnopqrstuvwxyz 1234567890

GOUDY OLD STYLE

ABCDEFGHIJKLMNOPQRSTUVWXYZ

abcdefghijklmnopqrstuvwxyz 1234567890

MODERN #20

ABCDEFGHIJKLMNOPQRSTUVWXYZ
abcdefghijklmnopqrstuvwxyz 12345678

OPTIMA

ABCDEFGHIJKLMNOPQRSTUVWXYZ
abcdefghijklmnopqrstuvwxyz 1234567890

PALATINO

ABCDEFGHIJKLMNOPQRSTUVWXYZ
abcdefghijklmnopqrstuvwxyz 1234567890

PALATINO ITALIC

ABCDEFGHIJKLMNOPQRSTUVWXYZ
abcdefghijklmnopqrstuvwxyz1234567890

BODONI BOOK

ABCDEFGHIJKLMNOPQRSTUVWXYZ
abcdefghiklmnopqrstuvwxyz   1234567890

BOOKMAN

ABCDEFGHIJKLMNOPQRSTUVWXYZ
abcdefghijklmnopqrstuvwxyz   1234567890

BERNHARD ROMAN

ABCDEFGHIJKLMNOPQRSTUVWXYZ
abcdefghijklmnopqrstuvwxyz 1234567890

CENTURY SCHOOLBOOK

ABCDEFGHIJKLMNOPQRSTUVWXYZ
abcdefghijklmnopqrstuvwxyz 1234567890

CLOISTER

ABCDEFGHIJKLMNOPQRSTUVWXYZ
abcdefghijklmnopqrstuvwxyz23456789

CRAW MODERN

ABCDEFGHIJKLMNOPQRSTUVWXYZ
abcdefghijklmnopqrstuvwxyz123456789

SOUVENIR LIGHT

ABCDEFGHIJKLMNOPQRSTUVWXYZ
abcdefghijklmnopqrstuvwxyz1234567890

TIMES ROMAN

ABCDEFGHIJKLMNOPQRSTUVWXYZ
abcdefghijklmnopqrstuvwxyz1234567890

WEISS ROMAN

ABCDEFGHIJKLMNOPQRSTUVWXYZ
abcdefghijklmnopqrstuvwxyz 2345678

CLARENDON LIGHT

ABCDEFGHIJKLMNOPQRSTUVWXYZ
abcdefghijklmnopqrstuvwxyz 2345678

FUTURA LIGHT

ABCDEFGH IJKLMNOPQRSTUVWXYZ
abcdefghijklmnopqrstuvwxyz
1234567890

CALEDONIA

ITC Typefaces

The International Typeface Corp. (ITC) was formed in 1970 by Ed Rondthaler (who has been called the "father of photolettering" because he has done more than anyone to develop photo-lettering) and Aaron Burns and Herb Lubalin, two of the foremost graphic designer/typographers. ITC designs contemporary new type styles and licenses them to many manufacturers of typographic services, cost-free, with a royalty arrangement wherein the designer of the ITC face gets a percentage of the royalty. The styles are marketed worldwide. ITC helped diminish the pirating of styles by many manufacturers who would steal designs indiscriminately, giving them new names and offering no recompense to the designer of the style.

ITC has contributed much to the development of new contemporary type styles for both text and display. All are in very good taste.

An ITC review board meets regularly to evaluate new alphabet styles. Any designer can submit samples. They also publish a quarterly, U&lc, an exciting graphics-oriented publication that every designer should read.

ITC Avant Garde Gothic was their first style. Some other ITC styles are shown on the next page.

AVANT GARDE GOTHIC BOOK

ABCDEFGHIJKLMNOPQRSTUVWXYZ

abcdefghijklmnopqrstuvwxyz 1234567890

(&.,„;!?'`"''--*$¢%/ ()/\\/¡¿[]‹›"˚˘ˆ˜˙~#£)

ALTERNATE CHARACTERS

AA CA C EA FA R GA HT KA LA LA LL MM NT Ø OE R R
R ASS ST ST T TH UT V VV VV WA T Q E C I M N R
æ c e ff fi ffi fl ffl Ø œ v v vv y

ALL ITC TYPEFACES COME IN MANY WEIGHTS. MOST HAVE OBLIQUE OR ITALIC VERSIONS.

Barcelona Medium	abcdefghijklmnopqrstuvwxyz ABCDEFGHIJKLMNOPQRSTUVWXY	**A**
Bauhaus Medium	abcdefghijklmnopqrstuvwxyz ABCDEFGHIJKLMNOPQRSTUVWXYZ	ß
Bookman Medium	abcdefghijklmnopqrstuvwxyz ABCDEFGHIJKLMNOPQRSTUVWX	**C**
Eras Demi	abcdefghijklmnopqrstuvwxyz ABCDEFGHIJKLMNOPQRSTUVWXYZ	**E**
Fenice Regular	abcdefghijklmnopqrstuvwxyz ABCDEFGHIJKLMNOPQRSTUVWXYZ	F
Lubalin Graph Medium	abcdefghijklmnopqrstuvwxyz ABCDEFGHIJKLMNOPQRSTUVWX	**G**
Serif Gothic Extra Bold	abcdefghijklmnopqrstuvwxyz ABCDEFGHIJKLMNOPQRSTUVWXYZ	**B**
Zapf Chancery Light Italic	*abcdefghijklmnopqrstuvwxyz ABCDEFGHIJKLMNOPQRSTUVWXYZ*	*E*

Numbers

Early counting was done with fingers.

One, two, three, and four were I, II, III, and IIII, which later became IV. The outline of the hand formed a V, representing five. Two Vs became an X for ten. The Romans extended this system to include other letters as shown in the diagram.

V	X	L	C	D	M
5	10	50	100	500	1000

At the end of the tenth century, the Arabs brought to Spain, from India, Arabic numerals, which we use today. These did not replace Roman numerals until the sixteenth century, however.

Numbers that represent succession are called ordinal: 1st, 2nd, 3rd, etc.

All numbers (except 1) are the same width visually. Zeroes are not as wide as the capital letter O in a type font.

There are two major forms of numerals, nonranging and ranging.

OPTIONAL

1234567890

These are nonranging (nonaligning or old style). The 3, 4, 5, 7, and 9 drop below the base line, whereas the 6 and 8 and sometimes the 2 extend above. There is an affinity between these numerals and old-style type fonts and lower-case.

1234567890

These are ranging (lining or modern) They all align between two lines. These numerals go with modern type styles and capitals.

Picking A Typeface

At some point in the creation of a typographic layout, the designer must choose a type style. In the past the rule was, "When in doubt, use Caslon." This may still be the answer in some cases. Many other factors may, however, help you determine what style of type to use. Some are listed here, in no particular order.

1. Does the type help express the mood or spirit of the message most forcibly? It should. If not, pick a safe, legible style.

2. Will the type fit the allotted space on the layout? If not, make adjustments — smaller-size type, more or less leading, different measure.

3. Is the typeface available? All printers do not have all styles. Check with your printer.

4. How will your type be printed? The same type looks different when printed by different processes (offset lithography, gravure, letterpress, silk screen, etc.). Also, what paper is it to be printed on?

5. Is the copy interesting? If not, the best layout and type selection will not help much.

6. Is the type the right size for the reader? The design may appeal to children or to an older audience, in which case the size and weight of the type are important.

7. How much will the type cost? Cost is always a factor, unfortunately.

8. Will the chosen type attract attention and encourage reading? If not, choose one that will.

9. Is your chosen type contemporary? Instead of a timeworn face, pick one that is fashionable. Clothing and car styles change; so do type styles.

Design of Paragraph Mass

The lines of body copy can be organized with a common alignment in any of the ways shown below.

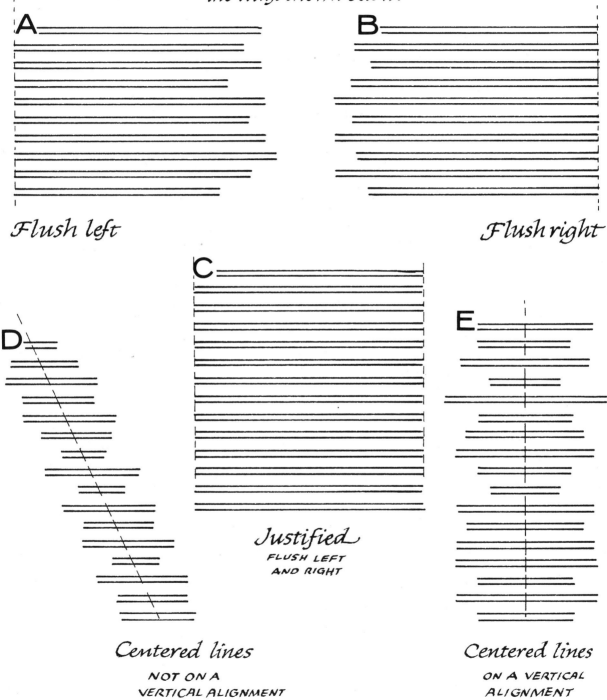

A

Flush left

B

Flush right

C

Justified

FLUSH LEFT AND RIGHT

D

Centered lines

NOT ON A VERTICAL ALIGNMENT

E

Centered lines

ON A VERTICAL ALIGNMENT

In some cases they may be organized in a mass that suggests a meaningful object, as in this example. ——————→

First draw a careful outline of the shape you want. Pick your type and find the character count per picas. Measure the count for each line and cast the entire copy to fit the shape. You will have to recast if you are long or short your first try. Change the size and/or leading to accommodate all the copy. Mark your manuscript, finally, with a slash mark / at the end of each line. Center all lines, mark specs, and send to the compositor.

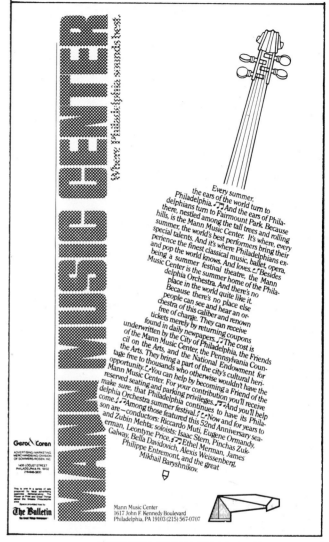

DESIGNER: TRACY CUNNINGHAM

SKETCH: HAL GREER

Text lines can cut around illustrations, as shown here. After type is set, cut the lines of the proof and position on the mechanical following the outline of the art.

Design of First Lines of Paragraphs in Ads

Different ways to design the first line of a paragraph are shown here. Designers should constantly observe how others have designed, or are designing, first lines in books, magazine ads, mailers, etc.

1. Indented first line.

On July 1, 1980, the 96th Congress passed the Motor Carrier Act of 1980, which had the effect of eliminating the value of operating rights carried on the books of all trucking companies. As a consequence, the

2. Overhanging indentation.

In order to acquaint you with paper and stationery, let's explore its history, then how paper is made, and lastly, the terms you will need to know in talking the language of stationery.

3. Stick-up initial (can be a large, decorative initial, as in old manuscripts).

Wetur adipscing elit, sed mod tempor incidunt ut labore et aliquam erat volupat. Ut enim ad quis nostrud exercitation ullamc nisi ut aliquip ex ea commodo vel eum irure dolor in reprehend esse molestaie son consequat, vel

THE LARGE CAP MUST ALIGN WITH ONE OF THE TEXT LINES.

4. Sunken initial.

I modo consequat. Duis au r in reprehenderit in volup estaie son consequat, vel nulla pariatur. At vero eos et dignissim qui blandit praesent

INITIAL MUST ALIGN TOP AND BOTTOM WITH TEXT LINES.

5. Use of device (see next page).

young women to become effective volunteers in the communities in which they live. Our members have served on the following civic and welfare agency boards; Children's Psychiatric Center, Inc., Community Services Council for

6. First two or three words in small caps.

AS WILL BE SEEN, each of the previously mentioned good typography and simplicity—all stem from strategy and all are achieved as the product of Whether that idea emerges from the typewriter, even—the Lord help us—from computerized product is style, not fashion.

Which gives us the hope that business bedraggled Cinderella creeping diffidently continue to walk resolutely down the Avenue.

In fact, our dream is that one day a perfume challenge his agency with:

7. First small sentence in italics.

Nam liber a tempor cum. Et harum in reprehenderit in voluptate velit consequat, vel illum dolore eu fu vero eos et accusam et justo blandit praesent lupatum delenit molestais exceptur sint occaecat dent, simil tempor sunt in culpa mollit anim id est laborum et dolor dereud facilis est er

8. First phrase in boldface (can be a different style from text type).

Hanc ego cum tene illum dolore tempor cum soluta nobis eligend quod a impedit anim id quod possim omnis es voluptas dolor repellend. Temporem office debit aut tum rerum necessit ut er repudiand sint et molestia Itaque earud rerum hic tenetury aut prefer endis dolorib asperiore

9. First large initial or word in color.

Nuos dolor et molestais exc occaecat cupidat non provident, in culpa qui officia deserunt mollit laborum et dolor fugai. Et harumd er expedit distinct. Nam liber a nobis eligend optio comque nihil anim id quod maxim placeat facer voluptas assumenda est, omnis

10. Hand-lettered lead-ins.

You will save more accusam odio dignissim qui blandit praesent aigue duos dolor et molestais excep cupidat non provident, simil tempo officia deserunt mollit anim id est lab fugai.

11. Ellipsis beginning.

...young women to become effective volunteers in the communities in which they live. Our members have served on the following civic and welfare agency boards; Children's Psychiatric Center, Inc., Community Services Council for Monmouth County, Family and Children's Service, Inc., Long Branch Public

Achieving Emphasis

The most common methods of emphasizing a word or phrase are shown below.

1. Boldface

Assistance is available in type selection, styling, layout and copy preparation for offset, photo engraving, electrotyping or printing **directly from type.** We offer a wide selection of foreign language accents and the skill and experience

2. Italic

Assistance is available in type selection, styling, layout and copy preparation for offset, photo engraving, electrotyping or printing *directly from type.* We offer a wide selection of foreign language accents and the skill and experience

3. Underscore

The quick <u>brown</u> <u>fox</u> jumps over the lazy dog

4. Size

Ink-smudged **hands** with nimble fingers,

5. Devices and directional elements

● **Excellence in typography is the result of nothing more than an attitude. Its appeal comes from the understanding used in its planning.**

6. Repetition

YANKEES VS. SOX
DOUBLEHEADER TODAY AT 2
YANKEES VS. SOX
DOUBLEHEADER TODAY AT 2

7. Color

A type for every need.

8. Simple borders

How should typography be evaluated?

9. Caps

Why can't we all be WINNERS?

10. Different style

CALL FOR SPECIAL OFFER!

11. Isolation

type

Temporem autem quinsud et aur tum rerum necessit atib saepe repudiand sint et molestia non Itaque earud rerum hic tenetury au aut prefer endis dolorib asperiore ego cum tene sentntiam, quid est eam non possing.

12. Slant

And we'll train your operator.

Sometimes extra space before and after a paragraph will set it off from adjacent paragraphs.

Bernard Shaw sometimes emphasized a word by giving it extra letterspace.

Most old style types are used extensively in fine bookwork because of their r e a d a b i l i t y and because they print well on book paper. Advertising designers who wish to give ...

Do not use emphasis on too many elements. "Too much is none."

Designing Large First Letters of Text

A large letter is often used as the beginning of a first paragraph. It is often a very bold letter. If it is a capital A, J, T, V, W, or Y, it can overhang slightly in the left margin of the text, so that it appears to line up with the text

Typesetting can actually cut costs because it uses less than half the space of typewritten copy. This can add up to tremendous savings in paper, printing, and postage cost.

Heretofore, to gain these benefits, copy had to be re-keyboarded for typesetting. A costly, time-consuming operation that could easily introduce new errors.

Wautem quinsud et aur office necessit atib saepe eveniet ut et molestia non este recusan rerum hic tenetury sapiente prefer endis dolorib asperiore ego cum tene sentntiam, quid ad eam non possing accomm

A different style for the cap or a large lowercase initial might also be used.

eem autem quinsud et aur tum rerum necessit atib saepe repudiand sint et molestia non Itaque earud rerum hic tenetury au aut prefer endis dolorib asper ego cum tene sentntiam, quid eam non possing accommodare paulo ante cum

Decorative material can surround the large capital.

How to Indicate Text Type on Layouts

The methods below can be used on rough or comprehensive layouts. Try to achieve an even tone (color) for the type mass.

1. *Double lines indicating the x-height of the type.*

2. *Solid, single strokes of a chisel-edge tool. The width of the chisel-edge is the x-height of the type.*

3. *Short and long strokes, as in 2, with breaks simulating word spacing.*

4. *Wiggley scribbles to simulate words.*

5. *Nonreading words lettered quickly. The weight of the strokes simulates the type. (This is called greeking).*

Azby ands enlpynog tzati teeters anz poliza zpta

6. *Use of transfer sheets. Greeking sheets of many styles are manufactured for use in indicating body copy in layouts.*

aut prefer endis dolorib asperiore repell cum tene sentntiam, quid est cur verear non possing accommodare nost ros quo ante cum memorite it tum etia ergat. No

7. *Photostat pieces of appropriate body type from your files. Paste the stats on your layout. The styles, weight, and spacing should approximate what you want on the layout.*

When using hand-drawn lines, as in 1, 2, and 3 above, stroke in a scratchy fashion by making your pencil or pen go back and forth. This simulates the look of the type in actual type.

Designing Display Headlines

The requirements of display in editorial typography are few and are not as demanding as "attention-getters" used in commercial typography. The guidelines demonstrated here are for commercial typography.

The focal point for printed matter is the headline. Many flamboyant styles were designed during the middle of the nineteenth century because of the industrial revolution and the resulting demands of competitive advertising. Although

colorful and dazzling, these styles, when used together, merely called attention to themselves rather than clearly communicating messages at a glance, which is really the primary function of a headline.

Display lines are usually larger and bolder than the accompanying body copy. The same type style often works well for both, but a headline style that contrasts greatly with the text style can also be used effectively.

Kabcdef Lghijkl

Lorem ipsum dolor sit amet, elit, sed diam nonnumy eiu labore et dolore magna enim ad minimim veniam ullamcorpor suscipit labor commodo consequat.

SAME TYPE STYLES

Kabcdef Lghijkl

Et tamen in busdad ne que nonor imper ned libiding cupiditat, quas nulla praid im minuiti potius inflammad dodecendense videantur, Inv santos ad iustitiami

CONTRASTING TYPE STYES

Every printed message has a type most appropriate for it. Some obvious examples are shown below.

TOO FAT? diet and reduce

ROMAN ARCHITECTURE

The Industrial Revolution

If two or more lines must be used, break the lines by sense.

Most old style
types are used
in fine bookwork because
they print well on
book paper.

BAD BREAK

Most old style types
are used
in fine bookwork
because they print well
on book paper.

THIS IS BETTER

Conserve space — two lines are better than three, and one is better than two. Fewer lines can be read more quickly.

A ═══
  ═══
  ═══

A ═══════
  ═══════

THIS IS BETTER

A ─────────────────

THIS IS BEST

If hand-lettered headlines are absolutely necessary, their style may be adapted from the style used in the text.

ANTIQUE SALE

Unfant aut inuiste fact est cond que neg facile efficerd possit duo conteud notiner si effecerit, et opes vel forunag veling en liberalitat magis em conveniunt. dabut tutungbene volent sib conciliant et, al is aptissim est ad quiet. Endium caritat praesert cum omning null siy

In computer photocomposition the letters of headlines frequently touch and even overlap slightly.

NEXT TIME TRY ALAN TEETERS

Transfer lettering sheets can be used for unusual display type arrangements.

A BEAUTIFUL CONDO

WITH SEA BREEZES

In addition to the examples just shown, the sample headings below show appropriate uses of type for headings.

1. All caps.

ALL ABOARD FOR FUNSVILLE

2. Only important letters are capped.

Every bite is a Taste Treat

3. All first letters of main words are capped.

International Flower Show

4. All lowercase letters.

secluded chalet in the mountains

5. Most important words made bolder. (same style).

IT'S **NOWe**© OR NEVER

6. *Most important words in different style.*

NEXT TIME TRY HIGGENBOTHAM

7. *Most important words all caps.*

It is used for JADE jewelry

8. *Most important words in italics.*

Ink-smudged hands with *calloused fingers*.

9. *Most important words in different tone or color.*

We have a best buy to shout about.

Many of the guidelines for organizing text type also apply to headlines. For example, legible types should be used for the most part.

The size of a heading can be influenced by the size of the page it is printed on.

Other suggestions for headings.

*Substituting an illustration for one
of the letters can add interest.*

W🌐RLD NEWS TONIGHT

JOINNOW $AVE MORE

ASAP IS FASTER

*Word spacing and letterspacing
of type in headlines should be tight.*

International Association of Platemakers

*Any type style can be used for any
kind of an ad.*

Acme Steel invites you to a party

*The designer should use his or her
judgment in choosing the type style
that best communicates the spirit
of the design.*

Display type is available in thousands of styles, many, many more than text type.
Here are some of the most common styles used for headings today. They come in different weights, and most have italics.

ABCDEFGHIJKLMNOPQRSTUVWXYZ
abcdefghijklmnopqrstuvwxyz 12345678
BODONI BOLD

ABCDEFGHIJKLMNOPQRSTUVWXYZ
abcdefghijklmnopqrstuvwxyz 234567
COOPER BLACK

ABCDEFGHIJKLMNOPQRSTUVWXYZ
abcdefghijklmnopqrstuvwxyz 23456789
CENTURY SCHOOLBOOK BOLD

ABCDEFGHIJKLMNOPQRSTUVWXYZ
abcdefghijklmnopqrstuvwxyz 1234567890
CHELTENHAM BOLD

ABCDEFGHIJKLMNOPQRSTUVWXYZ
abcdefghijklmnopqrstuvwxyz 1234567890
TIMES ROMAN BOLD

ABCDEFGHIJKLMNOPQRSTUVWXYZ
abcdefghijklmnopqrstuvwxyz 234567890

STYMIE BOLD

ABCDEFGHIJKLMNOPQRSTUVWXYZ
abcdefghijklmnopqrstuvwxyz 2345678

OPTIMA SEMIBOLD

ABCDEFGHIJKLMNOPQRSTUVWXYZ
abcdefghijklmnopqrstuvwxyz 2345678

LYDIAN BOLD

ABCDEFGHIJKLMNOPQRSTUVWXYZ
abcdefghijklmnopqrstuvwxyz 234567

FRANKLIN GOTHIC WIDE

ABCDEFGHIJKLMNOPQRSTUVWXYZ
abcdefghijklmnopqrstuvwxyz 234567

HELVETICA BOLD

ABCDEFGHIJKLMNOPQRSTUVWXYZ
abcdefghijklmnopqrstuvwxyz 234567

DOM BOLD

ABCDEFGHIJKLMNOPQRSTUVWXYZ

abcdefghijklmnopqrstuvwxyz 1234567890

WINDSOR

ABCDEFGHIJKLMNOPQRSTUVWXYZ

abcdefghijklmnopqrstuvwxyz 23456789

CRAW CLARENDON

ABCDEFGHIJKLMNOPQRSTUVWXYZ

abcdefghijklmnopqrstuvwxyz 123456789

TIFFANY MEDIUM

ABDEGIJKMQRSWXZ

abcdefghjkmopqrstvxyz

123456780

WIDE LATIN

ABCDEFGHIJKLMNOPQRSTUVWXYZ

COLUMNA (SOLID) CAPS ONLY

ABCDEFGHIJKLMNOPQRSTUVWXYZ

abcdefghijklmnopqrstuvwxyz 1234567890

PALATINO SEMIBOLD

ABCDEFGHIJKLMNOPQRSTUVWXYZ
abcdefghijklmnopqrstuvwxyz23456

ALTERNATE GOTHIC # 2

ABCDEFGHIJKLMNOPQRSTUVWXYZ
abcdefghijklmnopqrstuvwxyz 234567

20TH CENTURY ULTRABOLD ITALIC

ABCDEFGHIJKLMNOPQRSTUVWXYZ

MACHINE

ABCDEFGHIJKLMNOPQRSTUVWXYZ
abcdefghijklmnopqrstuvwxyz23

OLIVE ANTIQUE BLACK

ABCDEFGHIJKLMNOPQRSTUVWXYZ
abcdefghijklmnopqrstuvwxyz 234567

STYMIE EXTRABOLD ITALIC

ABCDEFGHIJKLMNOPQRSTUVWXYZ

FRANKFURTER

ABCDEFGHIJKLMNOPQRSTUVWXYZ
abcdefghijklmnopqrstuvwxyz 2345678

EUROSTILE BOLD

AABCDEFGHIJKLMNOPQRRSTUVWXYZ
aabcdeffghijklmnopqrrsttuvwxyyz 2345678

ABCDEFGHIJKLMNOPQRSTUVWXYZ
abcdefghijklmnopqrstuvwxyz1234567

ABCDEFGHIJKLMNOPQRSTUVWXYZ
abcdefghijklmnopqrstuvwxyz 12345678

ABCDEFGHIJKLMNOPQRSTTUVWXYZ
abcdefghijklmnopqrstuvwxyz1234567890

AbCDEFGHIJKLMNOPQRSTUVWXYZ
1234567890

ABCDEFGHIJKLMNOPQRSTUVWXYZ
abcdefghijklmnopqrstuvwxyz 1234567890

ABCDEFGHIJKLMNOP2RSTUVWXYZ
abcdefghijklmnopqrstuvwxyz 1234567890

BRUSH

ABCDEFGHIJKLMNOPQRSTUVWXYZ
abcdefghijklmnopqrstuvwxyz1234567

BODONI OPEN

ABCDEFGHIJKLMNOPQRSTUVWXYZ
abcdefghijklmnopqrstuvwxyz 12345

AMERICANA

ABCDEFGHIJKLMNOPQRSTUVWXYZ
abcdefghijklmnopqrstuvwxyz 1234567890

TRUMP MEDIAEVAL

ABCⱭDEEFᵹGHⱧIJKLⱩMNOPQRSSTⱩUUWXYZ
abcⱨdeᵹfᵹhijklmmnopqrꞨstuvwxyz 1234567890

ART GOTHIC

ABCDEFGHIJKLMNOPQRSTUVWXYZ
1234567890

LINING PLATE GOTHIC

ABCDEFGHJKLMNOPQRSTUVWXYZ
abcdefghijklmnopqrstuvwxyz 2345678

ABCDEFGHIJKLMNOPQRSTTUVWXYZ
abcdefghijklmnopqrstuvwxyz 1234567

ABCDEFGHIJKLMNOPQRSTUVWXYZ
abcdefghijklmnopqrstuvwxyz 1234567890

ABCDEFGHIJKLMNOPQRSTUVWXYZ
abcdefghijklmnopqrstuvwxyz 234567

ABCDEFGIJKLNPQRSTUVXYZ

ABCDEFGHIJKLMNOPQRSTUVWXYZ
abcdefghijklmnopqrstuvwxyz

abcdefghijklmnopq
qrstuvwxyz12345678

ABCDEFGHIJKLMNOPQRSTUVWXYZ
abcdefghijklmnopqrstuvwxyz 23456

ABCDEFGHIJKLMNOPQRSTUVWXYZ
abcdefghijklmnopqrstuvwxyz 1234567890

ABCDEFGHIJKLMNOPQRSTUVWXYZ
abcdefghijklmnopqrstuvwxyz 23456

ABCDEFGHIJKLMNOPQRSTUVWXYZ
abcdefghijklmnopqrstuvwxyz1234567890

ABCDEFGHIJKLMNOPQRSTUVWXYZ 1234567890

ABCDEFGHIJKLMNOPQRSTUVWXYZ
1234567890

PRISMA

ABCDEFGHIJKLMNOPQRSTUVWXYZ
1234567890

CARTOON BOLD

ABCDEFGHIJKLMNOPQRSTUVWXYZ
abcdefghijklmnopqrstuvwxyz 123456789

UNIVERSITY ROMAN

ABCDEFGHIJKLMNOPQRSTUVWXYZ
1234567890

BROADWAY

ABCDEFGHIJKLMNOPQRSTUVWXYZ
abcdefghijklmnopqrstuvwxyz 234567

HOBO

ABCDEFGHIJKLMNOPQRSTUVWXYZ 12345678

LIBRA

ABCDEFGHIJKLMNOPQRSTUVWXYZ
11234567890

MICROGRAMMA

ABCDEFGHIJKLMNOPQRSTUVWXYZ
abcdefghijklmnopqrstuvwxyz234567890

BAKER SIGNET

ABCDEFGHIJKLMNOPQRSTUVWXYZ

OPEN ROMAN CAPS

ABCDEFGHIJKLMNOPQRSTUVWXYZ

NEULAND

ABCDEFGHIJKLMNOPQRSTUVWXYZ
abcdefghijklmnopqrstuvwxyz123456789

PHENIX

How to Comp a Display Headline

When composing a display headline on a layout, first draw a straight pencil line on the back of a sheet of tissue.

Turn the tissue over, align the pencil line with the characters of type on the specimen sheet, and carefully draw your headline, moving the sheet back and forth to letterspace and compose your headline.

TISSUE

ALTERNATE GOTHIC NO. 2

72 point

ABCDEFGHI
JKLMNO
STU
abc

When finished, turn the tissue and erase the pencil line from the back.

Check the alignment of all letters with your Tsquare and correct alignment if necessary. Continue to develop the rest of your layout, or trace this heading onto a layout you have already started.

Typographic Devices

Unembellished paragraphs of type are most readable, but sometimes typographic devices are used to add interest or emphasis to a paragraph of text. These devices are available from all type houses, and you should have specimens of them handy. You must use discretion, however, for too many devices used at one time can be disastrous: they will clutter your job and detract from readabililty.

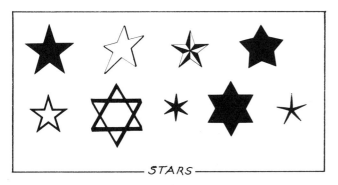

STARS

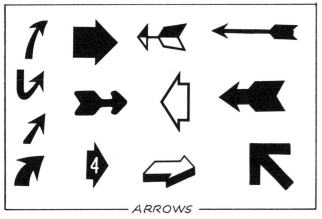

ARROWS

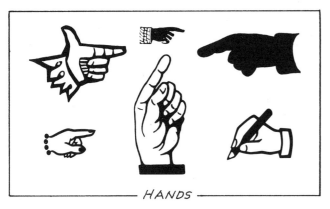

HANDS

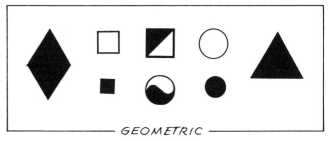

GEOMETRIC

ASTERISKS

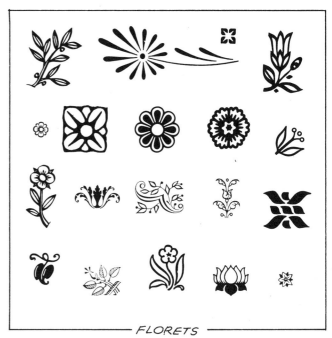

FLORETS

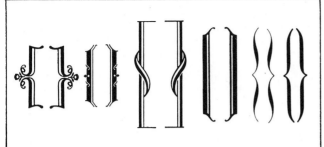

BRACKETS

FLOURISHES

MISCELLANEOUS

87

Many other ornamental typographic accessories (sometimes called dingbats, sorts, typecuts, astronomical signs, old style engravings, signs and symbols, fraternal emblems, and adcuts) are available.

Borders

Shown here are a few of the numerous typographic borders that are available. Parts of borders can be used decoratively as separations between paragraphs of text or between display and text.

Single-rule borders or combinations of rules of different weights can be used effectively.

Copy-fitting

Copy-fitting, copy casting, marking up, and casting off all mean the same thing: calculating your manuscript text to fit your layout. Before you order the type to be composed for this layout, you must calculate it so that it fits. This procedure is not complicated, but it does involve some simple arithmetic.

1. Character count

First count all the characters in your manuscript. All word spaces are to be included in your total. Your manuscript will be typewritten in one of three sizes. The characters that are ten to an inch are typed in pica size. When there are twelve characters to an inch, the type is called elite. Some typewriters today use characters that space differently than pica and elite, and for these you will have to count the characters per inch.

The following procedure is the same for all sizes of typewritten copy. Before typing the manuscript, tell the typist to try to make all lines the same length. Copy should be double-spaced in one column. The copy should be about six inches wide and slightly

to the right on 8½-by-11-inch white paper.

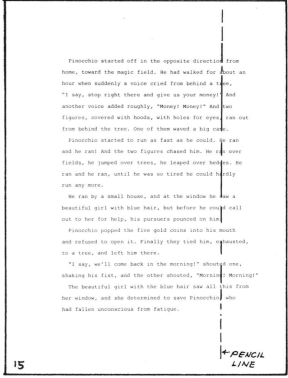

SMALL SCALE MANUSCRIPT PAGE

Find the shortest long line, and draw a vertical pencil line through all copy, from top to bottom. You can use a piece of tracing paper to make your calculations if you want to keep the original clean. Count the characters in one line up to the pencil line. Multiply this by the number of lines. Add all those extra characters to the right of the line and in the short lines. This will give you the total number of characters in one page of manuscript.

2. Fitting

Now choose a type style and size. On layout measure, in picas, the length of one line. Determine how many characters of the chosen type will fit this line. Most type specimen sheets will have a characters-per-pica table that will make this easier for you.

PICAS:	10	12	14	16	18	20	22	24	26	28
6 pt.	38	46	53	61	69	77	85	92	100	107
8 pt.	31	38	44	50	56	63	70	76	83	88
9 pt.	30	36	42	48	54	60	66	72	78	84
10 pt.	27	33	38	44	49	55	60	66	72	77
11 pt.	25	30	35	40	46	51	56	61	66	72
12 pt.	23	28	32	37	42	46	51	56	61	68
14 pt.	21	25	30	34	38	43	47	52	56	60

This is a characters-per-pica table for Times Roman. Pica width of the line is given in boldface across the top. The left-hand column, also in boldface, is the point size of the type. By cross-indexing you can find the average number of characters of the type that will fit the measure. For example: there are 66 characters of 10-point Times Roman lower case in a 24-pica measure.

In electronic photocomposition the character count changes according to the letterspacing you want—tight, very tight, etc.

Multiply the characters-per-pica by the number of picas in one line. Divide this into the total character count of the manuscript you previously made, and you will get the number of lines of type necessary to accommodate your manuscript. Add leading according to legibility tables (shown on page 39), and check the area with your layout. If necessary, make such adjustments as using larger or smaller type, changing leading, or changing the measure of one line on your layout. After a few attempts, you will find the entire procedure becomes a very simple matter.

3. Marking up the copy

In the left margin of the manuscript, clearly write all your specifications as in the diagram.

These are instructions for the typesetter and include, in sequence, the size and leading, the complete name of the typeface (Bodoni bold condensed, not just Bodoni), upper case and/or lowercase (U/LC), and how you want the type aligned (flush right, flush left, justified, or centered). Bracket the appropriate copy and draw a line to its specs, which are ballooned. Also specify any special effects you want (indents, double leading between paragraphs, etc.). Where necessary, use proofreaders' marks for italics, boldface, unusual line breaks, etc. For computer photolettering specify letterspacing as loose, normal, tight, or very tight.

The marked-up copy now goes to the typesetter, who will send proofs for correction after setting the type.

Must have by Friday, Aug. 16 2 sets repros — do not set

Indent 1st lines of all paras. 2 ems.

12 pt. / 14 Times Roman u/lc X 24 picas tight word # Justified

Pinocchio started off in the opposite direction from home, toward the magic field. He had walked for about an hour when suddenly a voice cried from behind a tree, "I say, stop right there and give us your money!" And another voice added roughly, "Money! Money!" And two figures, covered with hoods, with holes for eyes, ran out from behind the tree. One of them waved a big cane.

Pinocchio started to run as fast as he could. He ran and he ran! And the two figures chased him. He ran over fields, he jumped over trees, he leaped over hedges. He ran and he ran, until he was so tired he could hardly run any more.

He ran by a small house, and at the window he saw a beautiful girl with blue hair, but before he could call out to her for help, his pursuers pounced on him.

Pinocchio popped the five gold coins into his mouth and refused to open it. Finally they tied him, exhausted, to a tree, and left him there.

"I say, we'll come back in the morning!" shouted one, shaking his fist, and the other shouted, "Morning! Morning!"

The beautiful girl with the blue hair saw all this from her window, and she determined to save Pinocchio, who had fallen unconscious from fatigue.

do not set

Send proofs to Ernie Thompson 25 Buttonwood place, NYC 696-5106

(15) — *delete*

Fun and Games with Words

The graphic designer may be called on to design logotypes, game names, titles for TV programs, movie titles, and sometimes words in ad headlines. Here are some unusual combinations where the position of the type reinforces the meaning of the words. Answers to the word pictures are at the bottom.

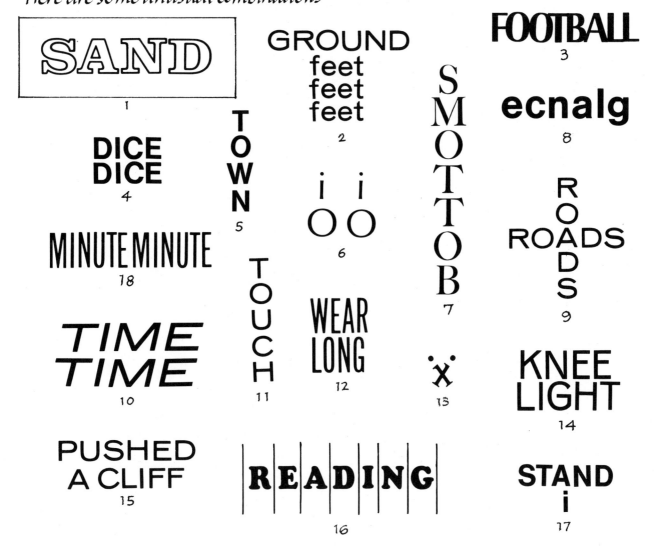

1. SAND BOX 2. THREE FEET UNDERGROUND 3. TOUCH FOOTBALL 4. PARADISE (PAIR OF DICE) 5. DOWNTOWN 6. CIRCLES UNDER THE EYES 7. BOTTOMS UP 8. BACKWARD GLANCE 9. CROSS ROADS 10. TIME AND TIME AGAIN 11. TOUCHDOWN 12. LONG UNDERWEAR 13. CROSS EYES 14. NEON LIGHT (KNEE ON LIGHT) 15. PUSHED OVER A CLIFF 16. READING BETWEEN THE LINES 17. I UNDERSTAND 18. MINUTE BY MINUTE

Making a Character Counting Scale

On one edge of a three-by-five-inch card, mark the count of the characters of the typed manuscript in divisions of five. Be sure the edge of the card is parallel to the typed copy. Label it "Typewriter", or "Manuscript."

Type shaped itself, we might say, accidentally. At first, it was based on manuscript forms probably with the intention of deceiving readers into the idea that the printed books were manuscript; whether that was the intention or not, it was the only way to make books readable to eyes accustomed only to m   that the   r con- cern

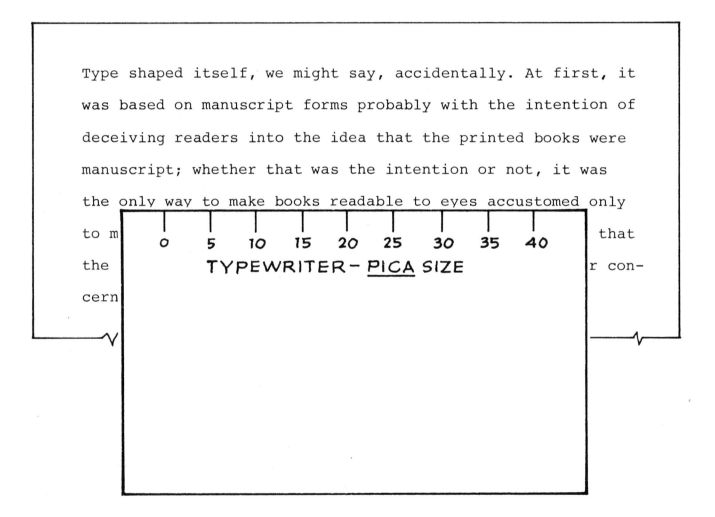

0   5   10   15   20   25   30   35   40

TYPEWRITER - PICA SIZE

You might also mark the size (elite or pica) of the typewriter and the style of the type you are specifying.

Turn the card and mark the opposite edge with a character count, also in units of five, of the type you have selected. You do this by laying the card on line with the size and style of type from a type specimen sheet. Label it "Type style" and note the size.

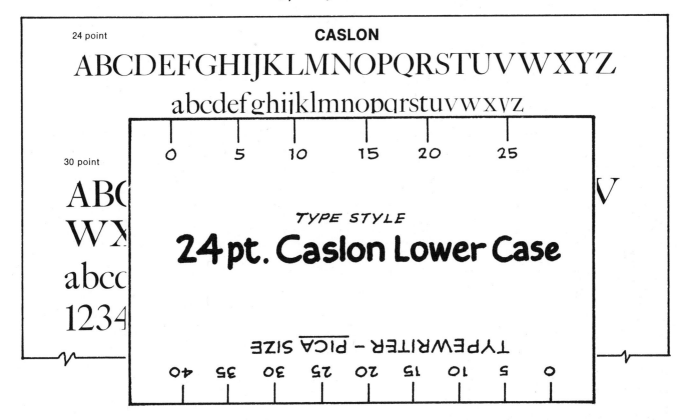

24 point

CASLON

ABCDEFGHIJKLMNOPQRSTUVWXYZ

abcdefghijklmnopqrstuvwxyz

30 point

```
ABC              V
WX
abc
1234
```

0 5 10 15 20 25

TYPE STYLE

24 pt. Caslon Lower Case

TYPEWRITER – PICA SIZE

40 35 30 25 20 15 10 5 0

If a particular type is used often, you should file it with other cards and use them over again. You will find them particularly helpful when counting on layouts with many measures of the same typeface. They will save you much valuable time.

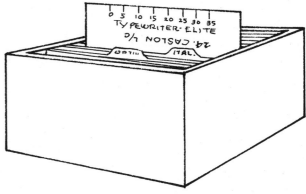

0 5 10 15 20 25 30 35
TYPEWRITER-ELITE
24. CASLON l/c
ROM.   ITAL.   ITAL.

Proofreaders' Marks

When proofs come back from the compositor, correct them if necessary and order reproduction (repro) proofs. The repro is then assembled into mechanicals of your layout, plates will be made, and the job will be printed. Final film proofs may be required for other purposes.

Shown below are correct proofreaders' marks used universally. Also shown is a sample of how a proof is marked for correction.

∧	CARET – MAKE CORRECTION INDICATED IN MARGIN
=	STRAIGHTEN TYPE; ALIGN HORIZONTALLY
‖	LINE UP VERTICALLY
ℛ	DELETE
#	INSERT SPACE
eq #	EQUAL SPACE BETWEEN WORDS OR LEADING
hr #	INSERT HAIR SPACE
ls	LETTERSPACE
¶	BEGIN NEW PARAGRAPH
no ¶	RUN PARAGRAPHS TOGETHER
☐	MOVE TYPE ONE EM FROM LEFT OR RIGHT
⊐	MOVE RIGHT
⊏	MOVE LEFT
⊐⊏	CENTER
⊓	MOVE UP
⊔	MOVE DOWN

tr	TRANSPOSE
(sp)	SPELL OUT
stet	LET IT STAND
⊥	PUSH DOWN TYPE
lc	LOWERCASE LETTER
cap	CAPITALIZE LOWERCASE LETTER
C+SC	SET IN CAPITALS AND SMALL CAPITALS
rom	SET IN ROMAN TYPE
bf	SET IN BOLD FACE TYPE
wf	WRONG FONT; SET IN CORRECT TYPE
×	RESET BROKEN LETTER
⟲	REVERSE (TYPE UPSIDE DOWN)
≡	UNDER WORD MEANS SET IN CAPITALS
=	UNDER WORD MEANS SET IN SMALL CAPITALS
—	UNDER WORD MEANS SET IN ITALIC
～～～	UNDER WORD MEANS SET IN BOLDFACE

⌄	INSERT COMMA
⌄	INSERT APOSTROPHE OR SINGLE QUOTATION MARK
⌄⌄	INSERT QUOTATION MARKS
⊙	INSERT PERIOD
(set)?	INSERT QUESTION MARK
;/	INSERT SEMICOLON
:/	INSERT COLON
|=|	INSERT HYPHEN
$\frac{1}{M}$	INSERT EM DASH
$\frac{1}{M}$	INSERT TWO-EM PARALLEL DASH
$\frac{1}{N}$	INSERT ONE EN DASH
[/]	INSERT BRACKETS
(/)	INSERT PARENTHESES
•••••	UNDER WORD MEANS LET IT STAND
✓✓✓	CORRECT SPACING
ℛ	DELETE AND CLOSE UP

It does not appear that the earliest printers had any method of correcting errors before the form was on the press/ The learned The learned correctors of the first two centuries of printing were not proof/readers in our sense/ they were rather what we should term office editors. Their labors were chiefly to see that the proof corresponded to the copy, but that the printed page was correct in its latinity that the words were there, and that the sense was right. They cared but little about orthography, bad letters or purely printers errors, and when the text seemed to them wrong they consulted fresh authorities or altered it on their own responsibility. Good proofs in the modern sense, were impossible until professional readers were employed / men who had first a printer's education, and then spent many years in the correction of proof. The orthography of English, which for the past century has undergone little change, was very fluctuating until after the publication of Johnson's Dictionary, and capitals, which have been used with considerable regularity for the past 80 years, were previously used on the miss or hit plan. The approach to regularity, so far as we have, may be attributed to the growth of a class of professional proof readers, and it is to them that we owe the correctness of modern printing. More errors have been found in the Bible than in any other one work. For many generations it was frequently the case that Bibles were brought out stealthily, from fear of governmental interference. They were frequently printed from imperfect texts, and were often modified to meet the views of those who published them. The story is related that a certain woman in Germany, who was the wife of a Printer, and had become disgusted with the continual assertions of the superiority of man over woman which she had heard, hurried into the composing room while her husband was at supper and altered a sentence in the Bible, which he was printing, so that it read Narr instead of Herr, thus making the verse read "And he shall be thy fool" instead of "and he shall be thy Lord." The word not was omitted by Barker, the king's printer in

Tips on Copy-fitting

Before the manuscript is written, you can tell the author how many words your layout can accommodate. Reverse the procedure just described to determine the number of characters (six letters to the average word).

Large first letters like T, W, V, and Y should overhang the left margin of text block.

Visit a composition house where type is set electronically. Ask questions.

Keep specs short and clear.

If manuscript has more than one page, number the pages at the top in correct sequence.

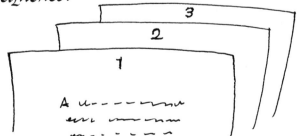

Make copies of all pages for your files.

Be sure stick-up or large first letter of first paragraph aligns with one of the text lines.

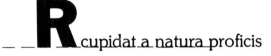

It may be creative to break the rules, but first be sure you know what they are.

When designing short lines, never spec wide word spacing.

Give indents in ems.

Carefully check all spelling and specifications in the manuscript before sending it out for composition.

Try to limit your use of text type to a few styles — some of the best designers use only a few.

Beware of using type as decoration. Type was made to be read and read easily.

Don't forget to specify typographic devices on your mark-up (bullets, rules, etc.).

Overhang all punctuation marks on the right margin of justified copy.

Send two copies of extra-long manuscripts to compositor. Two workers may be assigned to the job.

Avoid hyphenating two or more consecutive lines of justified type.

tters in fair propor-
to the same gener-
usic and poetry. Is

Cut in (kern) initial large stick-up letters, such as T, W, V, Y, F, and P, so that little letterspace occurs between the large initial and the next small letter of the text.

The act of setting

AA's cost money. PE's do not. Both cost valuable time.

Letterspacing should be the same for all copy. Word spacing can vary slightly, especially in justified type.

Never type manuscript on the front and back of a page.

Try to avoid marking your manuscript "RUSH."

When more than one correction occurs on a line, mark the corrections in sequence.

Corrections should be made just above the line.

Make corrections in red marker or ink.

Send layout, or copy, with specifications.

Don't forget to write the job number, your name, and company on every page of manuscript.

Job #2641
Karen Ueland
KIESTER & JONES, INC.

Meaningful shapes can be created with lines of text. Each line must be calculated and so marked.

Mark "the END" at the end of manuscript to be set.

Do not attach little notes to manuscript.

Never break a word at the bottom of a column or page.

Indicate when you must have proofs.

10/13 means 10-point type, 3-point leading.

In Europe, depth dimension is given first and width second. In the United States, dimensions are specified in the opposite manner.

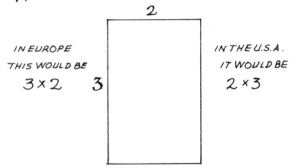

Footnotes and margin notes should be set two sizes smaller than text.

Flowers can be used for every occasion—to enhance your furnishings, decorate your table and inspire your party. Whichever way you like flowers, simplicity should be the keynote to good flower arranging. Everything is told here, from when to pick flowers and how to transport them, to drying

Decoration for the Table. Violet Stevenson. (Studio) Viking, 1965.

If your layout includes illustrations with captions, you may make the size of the caption type smaller than the text size.

designers who wish to give their copy a feeling

dability and because they print well on bo
wish to give their copy a feeling of age an
ce certain old-style faces have an appeara
re particularly suited to formal copy and di

Italic is good for setting dialogue, especially if it is brief.

Typewriter (Strike-on or Cold) Composition

The first patented typewriter in America, called a typographer, was designed by William Burt in 1829. It first produced embossed copy intended for the blind.

The first lettering designed for the typewriter was called pica. Today, most typewriters use pica type (ten characters per inch) or elite type (twelve characters per inch). All of the characters in each style take up the same amount of

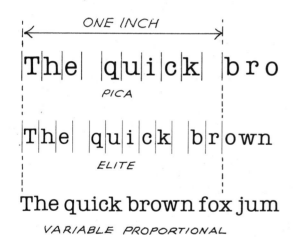

ONE INCH

The quick bro
PICA

The quick brown
ELITE

The quick brown fox jum
VARIABLE PROPORTIONAL

horizontal space. In 1935, type-writers were designed to use characters with variable proportional letterspacing. For example, an i would be two units wide and a w or an m would be five units wide. The IBM Executive is an example. The result is variable letter width like that of set type.

Many new styles have been designed since 1935, and the designer now can use a variety of typewriter styles for low-budget jobs such as inexpensive booklets and parts lists.

STANDARD TYPEWRITER
Imitation typewritten letters
place in the industrial world
who uses facsimile letters to

REMINGTON TYPEWRITER No. 2
Imitation typewritten letters
place in the industrial world
who uses facsimile letters to

UNDERWOOD TYPEWRITER INLAND
Imitation typewritten letters
place in the industrial world
who uses facsimile letters to

AMERICAN TYPEWRITER
Imitation typewritten letters have
place in the industrial world of to
who uses facsimile letters to promo

ELITE UNDERWOOD TYPEWRITER
Imitation typewritten letters have
place in the industrial world of to
who uses facsimile letters to promo

The text must be typed twice. A predetermined line width (measure) is marked with a vertical line, ⌐ and the copy is typed. Extra spaces for justified lines are added in retyping as shown in the diagram. ⌐

```
Type shaped itself, we might///
say, accidentally. At first, it
was based on manuscript forms//
probably with the intention of/
deceiving readers into the idea
that the printed books were////
manuscript; whether that was///
the intention or not, it was///
the only way to make books read-
able to eyes accustomed only to
manuscript pages. In a short///
time it became apparent that///
the considerations which con-//
trolled the scribe no longer///
concerned the printer.
```

```
Type  shaped  itself,  we  might
say,  accidentally.  At  first,  it
was  based  on  manuscript  forms
probably  with  the  intention of
deceiving  readers  into  the  idea
that   the   printed   books   were
manuscript;   whether   that   was
the   intention   or   not,   it   was
the  only  way  to  make  books read-
able  to  eyes  accustomed  only  to
manuscript  pages.   In   a   short
time   it   became   apparent   that
the  considerations  which  con-
trolled   the   scribe   no   longer
concerned the printer.
```

NOTE THE JUSTIFIED RIGHT HAND MARGIN ⌐

For unjustified text, a longest line, beyond which no character will run, must be determined. Text is typed accordingly. Some typewriters use high-speed electronic and CRT equipment where coded input is put on magnetic tape (MT). Corrections are made on another MT before final composition.

If you use a typewriter for composing text matter for inexpensive printings (throwaway circulars and the like), remove the fabric ribbon (on spools) and use sheets of carbon paper against the smooth typewriter paper. Be sure that the carbon faces the paper. The typed images will then be sharp and crisp, not ragged as in the example to the right. If you

ming

Enlarged photostat of letters typed through a <u>carbon</u> ribbon.

ming

Enlarged photostat of letters typed through <u>fabric</u> ribbon.

CARBON
PAPER

use one of the newer electric typewriters, get a carbon ribbon (either on spools or in a cassette). These ribbons are good only one time but are relatively inexpensive and will print 14,000 average words (more on some models). On some models the copy can be easily corrected as you type the text.

When you are finished typing carbon text, handle the completed sheets carefully. Gently spray them with workable fixative to prevent smudging.

You should clean the characters on the typewriter occasionally with a soft toothbrush and alcohol.

Variations of One Typeface

When a new typeface appears and becomes popularly accepted, variations of the style will be designed. In time a type style may add many variations: weight changes, italic, condensed and extended, and combinations of these. The entire range of a typeface is known as a family.

In 1947 Adrian Frutiger, a Swiss designer working in Paris, designed Univers. This type was unusual in that all its possible variations were designed from the outset. Univers is shown here to demonstrate all the changes possible for one typeface. Frutiger devised a numbering system to denote these variations. Univers 55 was the standard and

	Univers 45	Univers 46
Univers 53	Univers 55	Univers 56
Univers 63	Univers 65	Univers 66
Univers 73	Univers 75	Univers 76
Univers 83	Univers 85	

all other variations were based on it in units of ten. The higher the tens place, the bolder the type, so that 75 is bolder than 55. The ones place indicates how condensed the type is: the higher the number, the more condensed — 67 is more condensed than 63. All odd numbers are for roman and all even numbers are for italic.

Not all typefaces have this many variations. As their popularity increases, however, they may approach the number of Univers.

When designing with type, unity can be achieved by using one typeface for display and text in a layout. Interest is achieved by varying that face.

		Univers 39
Univers 47	Univers 48	Univers 49
Univers 57	Univers 58	Univers 59
Univers 67	Univers 68	

Univers 73 Open   Univers 67 Open   Univers 75 Open

Open letters were a later addition to the family.

Electronic Typesetting
A New Tool for the Graphic Designer

For over four hundred years following Gutenberg's invention of printing with movable type, all type was set by hand (foundry). During this time typographic terminology developed that we still use today (points, picas, ems, measures, etc.).

In 1884 a linecasting machine for setting type was inaugurated by Ottmar Mergenthaler. On his Linotype machine, an entire line of type could be cast in hot metal. Other companies followed with similar machines: Intertype, Monotype, and Ludlow.

In the 1960s electronic systems for setting type were developed, and computer-assisted phototypesetting began.

Today, many electronic systems are available to the graphic designers. What can be achieved on these machines staggers the imagination. The graphic designer must understand what these systems can do. Entire page makeups can be done on some systems, in which the designer may direct the programming or work closely with a specialist in a composition house.

A further development of computer-assisted typesetting is digital, without photographic assistance. Mark-up, coding, and paste-up may be eliminated in these systems.

Space limitations here do not allow exhaustive descriptions of these new systems. You should write to the companies for their literature. You will be surprised at how quickly you will understand what these systems can do.

To help you, listed below are a number of acronyms and technical terms relating to this new tool.

CAM - computer-assisted makeup
CG - computer graphics
Cluster - multiterminal systems
COM - computer output microfilms
CPS - characters per second
CPU - central processing unit
CRT - cathode-ray tube
Direct-input - system in which the typesetting device is connected to a keyboard

DOPES - digital offset plate exposure system
DP - data processing
EM - electronic mail
GTD - graphic display terminal
H&J - hyphenation and justification
Hard copy - any paper proof outputted from a computer system
Hardware - computer machinery
Interaction - communication between man and machine
Interfacing - to transfer data, in usable form, from one device to another
KRM - Kurzweil reading machine
Laser - an intense beam of light amplification caused by stimulated emission of radiation
LED - light-emitting diode
LPM - lines per minute
MCS - modular composition system
OBR - optical barcode recognition
OCR - optical character reader
Off-line - production of a "record" of information keyed
PIXEL - picture elements (of electronic and digital photograph)
PS - proportional spacing
QWERTY - any standard typewriter keyboard (position of the letters)
RAM - random-access memory
ROM - read-only memory

Software - computer programs (front-end)
Two-letter mnemonics - combination of letters associated with its meaning on a keyboard as in EJ, end of job; TY, typeface; BF, boldface; etc.
VDT - visual display terminal
WP - word processing

Digital Typesetting

The preliminary procedures for preparing type for printing are changing. Digital technology has been incorporated with traditional computer-assisted photographic typesetting. This technology makes it possible to do almost all graphic work (mechanicals, etc.) on a computer display screen, once the original art (type) is electronically scanned into a computer and converted into a digital code. In simple terms digitization is the development of a type character by building its shape out of a series of individual elements. The quality of the resulting typographic composition is of the highest, and the speed of setting is fantastic. A step-by-step procedure of digitization of a single type character is shown below. Forget, for the moment, the systems that use photographic negatives in their disks, matrixes, etc. Digital typesetting requires no photo unit.

The development of digitized type begins with an artist's drawing of each of the characters[1]. The character is described and exposed by an infinitesmal CRT (Cathode-Ray Tube) beam, which paints the character on photo material. The process is called scanning. The character is scanned to a sixty-four-point

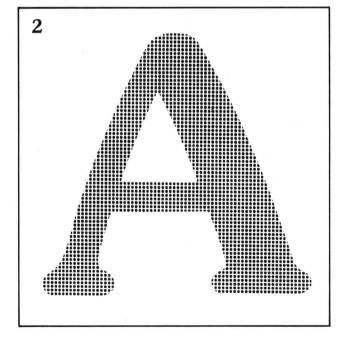

machine master character for optimum resolution. The scanner divides a specific area into tiny spaces or elements. These elements make up the scanning matrix[2]. The drawn character is placed on the matrix. The scanning mechanism reads the character, element by element. Those elements that lie within the body of the character are recorded on a computer disk. From this recorded digital information, the computer develops a mathematical outline of the character[3]. This outline enables the computer to instruct the CRT beam to paint vertical strokes on the photosensitive material, which start and stop at the points

dictated by the outline. These vertical strokes are the areas of photo exposure that combine to make up the typeset character in its final output form on photosensitive material[4]. Actually, the vertical strokes overlap to assure uniform photodensity.

CONTINUED ON NEXT PAGE

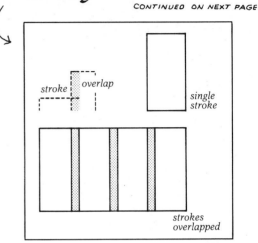

stroke   overlap

single stroke

strokes overlapped

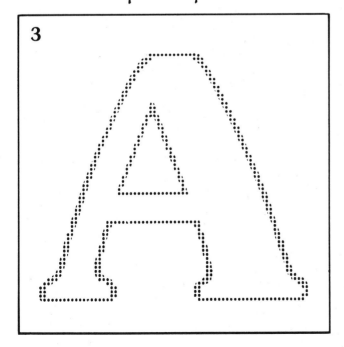

3

4

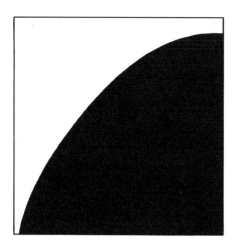

Edge definition of actual output enlarged to 640%.

A

Digital systems of typesetting are capable of setting type from five to seventy-two points. The range of sizes in between can be set in half-point increments. They also have reverse leading capability.

Moreover, these systems can modify the information for any one character to create a number of special effects.

hello

hello

hello

Computer-Assisted Phototypesetting

An advanced system of phototypesetting was introduced in the 1960s that uses a computer and cathode-ray tubes — CRT — your television is a cathode-ray tube. This system produces type on paper or film or directly onto paper printing plates at incredible speeds. Many companies manufacture a variety of systems. The machines are called hardware. Some systems are complete, while others assist other systems.

A simplification of the procedure for most systems, from the designer's mark-up to final proof follows:

1. The designer's copy is keyboarded manually, similar to typing on a typewriter. A display screen shows what the operator is typing while the copy is coded on a tape, disc, or card. Corrections can be made.

2. The tape, disc, or card is then programmed on a computer, which may also drive a photounit.

3. The photounit sets the type on paper or film.

4. The paper or film is then developed automatically on a processor. A proof is produced for checking.

5. The tape or film is then fed into a visual display terminal to delete or add copy and make additional corrections if necessary. It has a keyboard and a display screen. The corrected tape or disc goes back to the photounit for final proof.

Write to the manufacturers of the hardware for brochures and promotional material. After some confusion you will begin to understand this electronic technology. Go to a composing shop and see these systems at work. Visit trade shows. Ask questions.

Typographic Layout

Typography is an art. Communicating ideas, whether to sell a product or to provide information or entertainment, is its primary function. Visual appeal, loud or quiet, enhances this communication and is paramount in all typographic design.

One important aspect of visual appeal is layout. Good layout is the result of careful arrangement of all the required elements. Shown here are four basic layouts used today.

In a symmetrical layout, all elements are centered on an imaginary center line. From the time of Gutenberg to the late nineteenth century, almost all typographic layouts were symmetric.

←CENTER LINE

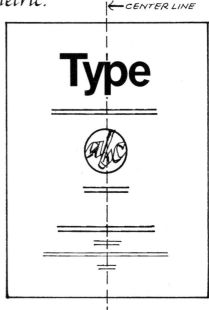

The industrial revolution and the resulting demands of competitive advertising led to another basic arrangement — asymmetry. The elements in an asymmetric layout are balanced but not symmetric as is shown.

In a flush left or flush right layout,
all elements align on the left or right,
with the opposite edge ragged.

This grid, or modular, arrangement originated in Switzerland.
There are many variations to this
layout.

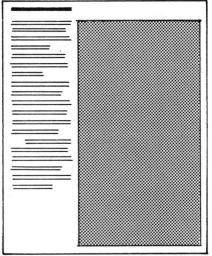

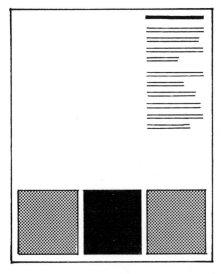

✳ The graphic artist must keep up
with contemporary art movements
to glean new ideas for layouts. Visit
museums, galleries, and art shows.

Read good graphic arts magazines.
They will not only be enlightening
experiences; they will give a feel for
the contemporary that is essential
to the competent graphic designer.

What Type Styles Express

Any type style can be used in any design providing the designer has a legitimate reason for using it — a reason that can be communicated easily to the reader. Many styles have been designed for specific uses — extra-bold sans serif caps attract attention on a poster, for example.

Most styles do express a certain mood or feeling. Aside from text types, which are designed for easy reading, the following list of styles generally express the accompanying associations or moods:

Old-style Roman: dignity, inscriptional, antique, classic, renaissance.

HISTORY OF ROME

Black Letter: printing, religion, certificates, diplomas, renaissance.

Certificate of Ownership

Victorian display style: uniqueness, circus, entertainment.

Formal script : announcements, invitations, grace, handwriting, personality, colonialism.

We teach you to write beautiful letters

Modern Roman: mechanical perfection, copper engraving, craftsmanship.

FINEST SWISS WATCHES

Square Serif: display, architectural subjects.

SKYSCRAPERS CONSTRUCTION CO.

Sans Serif: simplicity, the contemporary.

ELECTRONIC MASTERPIECES

Italics : speed, emphasis (when used with roman).

WE GET YOU THERE FASTER!

Typefaces Designed by the Author

Shown here are three typefaces designed by the author. The first, Gray Bulba, was originally designed for promotion of the motion picture "Taras Bulba" and was later included in the library of Photo Lettering Inc. An attempt was made to capture the ethnic flavor of Russia in the letter forms.

ABCDEF
GHIJKL
MNOPQ
RSTUVX
WYZ tf

TARAS
BULBA
YUL
BRYNNER
TONY
CURTIS

R
ñ
Q

The second typeface, Norcross #2, was designed for a greeting card company. It was one of the first joining formal-script types to be created for computer-assisted photolettering. Ligatures, combinations of two letters joined together, aided in getting a good join on otherwise difficult combinations.

qu th rr rs un
um ur us uv
an ar am as
er em es ev
on or os om

I'll be glad to
hold your hand
till you're well.

This typeface has been used on thousands of greeting cards.

a b c d e f g h i j k l m n o p q u r s t u v w x y z

s w r n u y rr rs en er es ev in ir is iv m ar as av th

ur us uv on or os ov br bs ss ! _ ? : ' . , ; ' -) (-

1 2 3 4 5 6 7 8 9 0 " " " . _

A B C D E F G H I J K L M N O P Q

R S T U V W X Y 3

COMPLETE FONT OF NORCROSS #2

The third type was designed for the 1976 Bicentennial. The letters were first hand-lettered and then repeated with photoprints to form a master sheet like the dry-transfer sheets on the market today. Adhesive spray was applied to the backs of sheets. This inexpensive method can be achieved by any enterprising letterer to create a new typeface. →

AMERICAN ANTIQUES

'76
AAAAABBBCCCC
DDDDEEEEEFFF
GGHHHHIIIIIJJK
KLLLLMMM NNN
NNOOOOOPPPQ
QRRRRRSSSSSTT
TTTUUUUVVWW
WXX YYYZZ A A
EELL MM NN &&
SS ,,..??!! "" "" - - - -

117

Dry-Transfer Type

Type on self-adhesive translucent sheets is available for unusual typographic effects that would be costly and time-consuming if set otherwise. Individual letters are cut from the sheet, which has repeats of all letters, and laminated onto illustration board to compose words. The letters can also be transferred to your design by pressure. These sheets are sold in most art supply stores as Letraset, Chartpak, Zipatone, and Formatt. Besides typefaces, all sorts of decorative devices are also available.

SMALL SCALE OF A LETRASET
SHEET OF DRY-TRANSFER TYPE.

A SHORT HISTORY OF FLYING

NERVOUS TENSION?

Because this type sometimes shrinks with time, get a photoprint or a sharp photostat of the line after designing it. Use the print, which will not shrink, on your mechanical.

DINE AT THE ROUND TABLE RESTAURANT

Previewing Your Ad

You can get a fair idea of what your layout will finally look like when it is printed in a magazine or newspaper before you go into final production by making a copy of your layout, trimming it to ad size, and pasting it onto a page of the magazine or newspaper. You can evaluate it and perhaps make changes. You may also want to show it to your client.

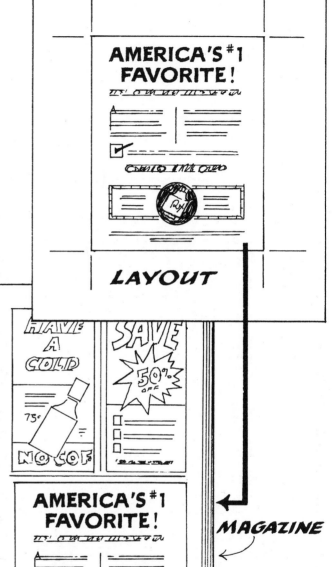

LAYOUT

MAGAZINE

Loose-Leaf Notebook Reference File

If you see unusual printed typographic layouts or new type-face showings or anything related to typographic excellence, file it in a loose-leaf notebook. This file will serve as a constant source of inspiration and may suggest a solution to a future design problem. The typographic scene is constantly changing, and items in the book can be easily replaced.

Make inexpensive copies of items from magazines or other printed pieces that others may still want to read.

fipunculo per ilquale emanaua laqua della fontana per artificio perpe,
tua in la fubiecta concha.

Nel Patore dunque di quefto uafo promineua uno pretiofiffimo mó
ticulo, mirabilmente congefto di innumere gemme globofe preffamente
una ad laltra coaceruate, cum inæquale, o uero rude deformatura, lepidif
fimamente il móticulo fcrupeo rendeuano, cú corrufcatióe di uarii fulge
tri di colore, cum proportionata eminétia. Nel uertice, o uero cacumine
di quefto monticulo, nafceua uno arbufculo di mali punici, di tronco, o
uero ftipite & di rami, & fimilmente tutto quefto compofito di oro prælu
cente. Le foglie appofitie di fcintilláte Smaragdo. Gli fructi alla granditu
dine naturale difperfamente collocati, cum il fidio doro ifchiantati larga
mente, & in loco degli grani ardeuano nitidiffimi rubini, fopra omni pa,
ragonio nitidiffimi di craffitudine fabacea. Pofcia lo ingeniofo fabro di
quefta inextimabile factura & copiofo effendo del fuo difcorfo
imaginario hauea difcriminato, in loco di Cico gli grani cum
tenuiffima bractea argentea. Oltra di quefto & ragioneuol,
mente hauea ficto & alcuni altri mali crepati, ma di
granelatura immaturi, oue hauea cópofito cum im,
probo exquifito di craffi unione di candore orienta,
le. Ancora folertemente hauea fincto gli balau
fti facti di perfecto coralio in calici pieni di api
ci doro. Vltra di quefto fora della fum,
mitate del fiftulatamente uacuo ftipite
ufciua uno uerfatile & libero fty,
lo, il cardine imo delqua
le, era fixo in uno ca,
po peronato, o ue
ramente firma
to fopra il medio
dellaxide. & afcendeua
per il peruio & inftobato trunco.

XEROX COPY OF TYPE – ALDUS MANUTIUS, 1499

Keep a page of addresses of graphic arts supply houses, telephone numbers of typographic services, etc.

Photo - Lettering INC. 25 W. 45
NYC 10036 575-0200

Herb Wiley, Lettering (get Phone #)
West chester, Pa. 19380

ATA 461 4th Ave. NYC 10001
Walter Dew

Include notes from lectures, random sketches, and accidental doodles that may have value sometime in the future.

Mrs. Goudy said:
"Basic fundamentals
are most important
LEARN
THEM"

Libby

Backword

This book has attempted to familiarize the graphic artist with the elements of typographic design. In the specific area of typesetting, revolutionary changes have occurred through the use of electronic aids. The computer may well be called a tool for the modern typographic designer. Perhaps the most significant tip in the book is for the designer to learn, as soon as possible, how computer-assisted photocomposition and digital generation of new type styles is accomplished. Find and carefully read books on the subject and brochures that are available from the manufactures of the electronic hardware. Actually see the systems at work, visit typesetting houses, and ask questions. The future graphic artist may do more designing at the keyboard of an electronic typesetting system than at the drawing board.

Despite these advances, however, what a reader reads — what a typographic artist creates — is a visual experience. The rules of typographic organization will always apply, even though the means of accomplishing the end result may change.

Today's typographic designer must keep abreast of the constantly changing scene. New visual concepts, new typefaces, new methods will appear, but the primary goal of the designer will continue to be a visually attractive design and an easily comprehended message.

Acknowledgments

A book such as this is rarely the result of one person's effort. Others, listed below, helped to make this book a reality, and I would like to thank them for their help. Thanks to my son, Tim, who typed the manuscript; to Ed Rondthaler, for permission to show ITC types; to Bob Gero, of Gero & Coren, Advertising, Marketing and Merchandising, Division of Somers/Rosen, Inc., Philadelphia, PA, for authorization to reprint the ad on page 61; to Walter Dew of ATA for permission to reprint the material on page 97; to Eliot B. Payson and the S. D. Warren Company, Division of Scott Paper Company for allowing me to use odds and ends from their publications; to Harry B. Zane and the Compugraphic Corporation, for help with the sections on digital typesetting; to Linda E. Rathjen, who was so helpful in editing all the copy; and finally to all the designers of typefaces and typographic designers — from Gutenberg to Zapf — for creating the thousands of typefaces we still use and for giving us a rich heritage of excellent typography upon which we can draw for our own work in communications today.

Bibliography

Carl Dair
DESIGN WITH TYPE
U. of Toronto Press, Toronto, Can.

Paterson and Tinker
HOW TO MAKE TYPE READABLE
Harper and Bros., N.Y.C.

Emil Ruder
TYPOGRAPHY
Hastings House, N.Y.C.

Leonard F. Bahr
ATA ADVERTISING PRODUCTION HANDBOOK
ATA of America, Inc., N.Y.C.

Milton Glaser
GRAPHIC DESIGN
Viking Press, N.Y.C.

Herbert Spencer
THE VISIBLE WORLD
Hastings House, 1961, N.Y.C.

Jan Tschichold
DESIGNING BOOKS
Wittenborn Schultz Inc., N.Y.C.

Allen Hulburt
PUBLICATION DESIGN
Van Nostrand Reinhold Co. Inc., N.Y.C.

Edward M. Gottshall
GRAPHIC COMMUNICATIONS 80'S
Prentice Hall, Inc. West Nyack, NY

Aaron Burns
TYPOGRAPHY
Van Nostrand Reinhold Co. Inc., N.Y.C.

Hermann Zapf
ABOUT ALPHABETS
M.I.T. Press, Cambridge, Ma

Stanley Rice
CRT TYPESETTING HANDBOOK
Van Nostrand Reinhold Co. Inc. N.Y.C.

Armin Hofman
GRAPHIC DESIGN MANUAL
Van Nostrand Reinhold Co. Inc., N.Y.C.

Stanley Morrison
FIRST PRINCIPLES OF TYPOGRAPHY
Cambridge U. Press, 1951

POCKET PAL
Graphic Arts Production
International Paper Co., N.Y.C.

James Craig
PHOTOTYPESETTING - A Design Manual
Watson-Guptill Publications, N.Y.C.

COMPUTER TERMS for the TYPOGRAPHIC INDUSTRY
International Typographic Composition Asso.
Washington, DC

Stanley Hlasta
PRINTING TYPES
and How to Use Them
Carnegie Press, Pittsburgh, Pa.

D. B. Updike
PRINTING TYPES; Their History, Forms and Use
Harvard U. Press, Cambridge, MA

Publications:

U&lc (Upper and lower case)   Art Direction
Communication Art (CA)   Graphic Arts Monthly
American Artist   TypeWorld

Free lists of books on typography and related subjects can be secured by writing to:

Pentalic Corporation, 132 West 22nd Street, New York, NY 10011
Dover Publications, INC., 180 Varick Street, New York, NY 10014
TypeWorld, 15 Oakridge Circle, Wilmington, MA 01887
John Neal, 608 5th Ave., Suite One, Greensboro, NC 27405
National Composition Asso. 1730 N. Lynn St., Arlington, VA 22209

Index